P9-CBA-543

Beyond Macaroni *and* Cheese

MOM-TESTED
KID-APPROVED
RECIPES

Edited by
Mary Beth Lagerborg
and
Karen J. Parks

ZONDERVAN™

GRAND RAPIDS, MICHIGAN 49530 USA

WWW.ZONDERVAN.COM

MOTHERS OF
M♥PS
PRESCHOOLERS

ZONDERVAN™

Beyond Macaroni and Cheese
Copyright © 1998 by MOPS International, Inc.

Requests for information should be addressed to:
Zondervan, *Grand Rapids, Michigan 49530*

Library of Congress Cataloging-in-Publication Data

Beyond macaroni and cheese: mom-tested, kid approved recipes / edited by Mary Beth
Lagerborg and Karen J. Parks.
    p.   cm.
  ISBN-10: 0-310-21978-7 (softcover)
  ISBN-13: 978-0-310-21978-1
    1. Cookery, American.   I. Lagerborg, Mary Beth.   II. Parks, Karen J.
TX715.B4937   1998
641.5973-dc 21   98-20277
                                                    CIP

All Scripture quotations, unless otherwise indicated, are taken from the *Holy Bible: New
International Version®*. NIV®. Copyright © 1973, 1978, 1984 by International Bible Society.
Used by permission of Zondervan. All rights reserved.

All rights reserved. No part of this publication may be reproduced, stored in a retrieval
system, or transmitted in any form or by any means — electronic, mechanical, photocopy,
recording, or any other — except for brief quotations in printed reviews, without the prior
permission of the publisher.

Published in association with the literary agency of Alive Communications, Inc., 7680
Goddard Street, Suite 200, Colorado Springs, CO 80920.

Interior illustrations by Don McLean
Interior design by Sherri L. Hoffman

Printed in the United States of America

---

07 08 09 10 /❖ DC/ 18 17 16 15 14 13

To the mom who scribbled this note on the back of a recipe:

My kids are in a rut.
All they like is
pizza
Mexican dish
mac cheese and hot dogs
pancakes
fried chicken (Kentucky — not mom's!)

I hope we will be able to find some new recipes
for our family in this cookbook.

Contents

❰ Acknowledgments ❱

To appreciate how many women's efforts have gone into the creation of this book, you must remember that each recipe represents a different contributor, and each handful of recipes represents a different recipe tester. Their names appear in the back of this book. Without their enthusiasm and their taking the time to find, copy, and send that one special recipe, there would be no *Beyond Macaroni and Cheese*.

We must thank our families. One day in the offices of MOPS (Mothers of Preschoolers) International, we told a colleague we were going to spend the day working on the cookbook. "What are you cooking?" she asked with a smile.

"Oh, this isn't about cooking," we replied, as we bustled off to shuffle piles and files, recipes and evaluations. Of course this book is very much about cooking, but at times in the compiling of it our own families have had to go without their daily bread — from us.

Then there is the support staff without which you would not be reading words on this page. Karen Hanson committed the book to computer, interfacing between two, sometimes cranky computers. After pulling an all-nighter entering recipes, Karen was still saying, "Oh, I'm having fun!" In addition, Mikki LeVett ("Marvelous Mikki") was our dependable helper and problem solver.

Writers are supposed to retreat to the Scottish moors or a South Sea island to write a book. We did have our moments, if not months, of escape, thanks to Carole Allen and Christy Holbrook, who opened their mountain homes to us.

Finally, thanks to all those who believed in this project and lent their crucial expertise and support: Elisa Morgan, Carol Kuykendall, Michele Hall, Gail Burns, Lynn Westdal, Brenda Quinn, Kelly Jacobson, and Teresita Ndibongo at MOPS International; Rick Christian of Alive Communications; and our terrific team at Zondervan Publishing House: Linda Peterson, Sandy Vander Zicht, Rachel Boers, Londa Alderink, and Kathy Bieber.

Hugs and chocolate to all.

❪ Introduction ❫

Something about the gray November morning drew Karen's thoughts back home to Oklahoma, to the childhood memory of her mother's kitchen and homemade macaroni and cheese. She smelled the rich aroma from the oven and imagined a brown crust forming on top and creamy cheese bubbling up through the vent holes.

Of course, her own children had never experienced this sensual delight. They knew only macaroni and cheese out of a bright blue box, that too yellow-orangy kind. So today Karen would share with them a piece of her childhood.

Pulling down her cookbooks, she searched for a *real* macaroni and cheese recipe. Why hadn't she copied her mother's? Guess it seemed too ordinary at the time, merely the carbohydrate accompaniment to Mom's meatloaf. Ah ha! Found one. Four cheeses. Mustard. White sauce. They'd love it.

Tommy, age 5, and Daniel, age 2, helped Karen grate the cheese. Seven-year-old Kate helped her pour macaroni into the boiling water.

By the time they sat down to dinner, the kids had heard many stories from Grandma Dodo's kitchen. Rather than serve it at the stove, Karen brought the oozing casserole to the table and triumphantly set it in the center. It was rich, creamy, and . . .

" . . . too white, Mommy. It's too white. This isn't macaroni and cheese!"

The three kids peered at their steaming, lumpy white mounds. Each tried a forkful, gamely, for Mom's sake, but no one except Karen enjoyed it.

In a week or so they would return to the bright blue box. But Karen's memories survived intact, with a new one she would laugh over in time.

Sometimes Karen grabs the bright blue macaroni box because that's all the cooking the day will bear — or the only thing she has on hand. Other days Karen journeys down the road beyond macaroni and cheese to explore new dishes, some of which will be "experiences," but others that will become family favorites.

In this cookbook, we invite you to lift your sights to the horizon beyond macaroni and cheese. Realizing there are some days when the boxed variety is "what works," venture to also try new dishes. Dare to have company sometimes, or to take a meal to a friend.

We want you to think of this book as your friend. So, to help you on your journey, we've included tips and tidbits, each with its own identifying icon.

Your guide into the "land beyond" is Evey, for Every Mom. She could be your neighbor, sister, mother, or friend, who has come to sit in your kitchen and keep you company while you cook. Evey wants to make your time in the kitchen easier, sometimes speedier, and more fun.

Since part of the joy of cooking is having a buddy, we'll suggest ways you can involve young helpers in the kitchen, or ways you can constructively occupy them so you can cook by yourself.

The breaking of bread together is a time for families to give thanks and reflect on the occupations of the day. So we also give a sampling of Scriptures and table graces.

Moms shared with us their kitchen catastrophes, which we pass on to you. Whatever the worst that has befallen you in the kitchen, take heart: you are not alone.

Two final icons help to defuse anxiety from the process of having company and enable you to more easily take a dish to a potluck, or meals to a friend.

Each of the recipes in *Beyond Macaroni and Cheese* was provided and tested by moms involved in a network of support groups called MOPS, or Mothers of Preschoolers. Their families liked the recipes, and we think yours will too.

Key to Icons

 Tips from Evey — your neighbor, sister, mother, or friend

 Kids can keep you crazy in the kitchen, or they can help you like this. . . .

 A sampling of Scriptures and table graces

 Kitchen catastrophes we have known . . . in case you thought yours were unique

 Company-caliber dishes and tips to wow your in-laws and friends

 Dishes that travel to potlucks or friends

Macaroni and Cheese

Ingredients:

½ lb. macaroni
1 T. butter
1 egg, beaten
1 tsp. salt
1 tsp. dry mustard
1 T. hot water
3 c. grated sharp cheese
1 c. milk
½ c. seasoned croutons, crushed

Directions:

1. Preheat oven to 350°.
2. Boil macaroni in water until tender and drain thoroughly.
3. Stir in butter and egg; mix mustard and salt with hot water and add to macaroni.
4. Add cheese, leaving enough to sprinkle on the top.
5. Pour into a buttered 2-quart casserole dish; add milk, sprinkle with cheese and seasoned croutons. Bake for about 45 minutes, or until the custard is set and the top crusty. Serves 8.

In case you are overtaken by the urge to create homemade Macaroni and Cheese for your family, try this recipe. In a taste test of ten different recipes, it was the clear winner.

The Born Loser reprinted by permission of Newspaper Enterprise Association, Inc.

Bountiful Plains

of

BREAKFASTS, BRUNCHES, AND BREADS

Grandma McGee's Corn Bread

Ingredients:

1 c. cornmeal (preferably stoneground)
¾ c. flour (preferably whole wheat)
2 tsp. baking powder
1 tsp. salt
½ c. powdered milk
¼ c. wheat germ
2 eggs, well beaten
1 c. buttermilk
¼ c. water
½ c. small cheddar cheese chunks

Directions:

1. Preheat oven to 450°.
2. Mix dry ingredients together. In another bowl combine wet ingredients.
3. Stir all together until well blended; stir in cheddar cheese.
4. Pour into a greased round cake pan and bake 25 minutes.

 Try Grandma McGee's Cornbread for breakfast toasted with butter and honey or syrup.

 This trio is good to have on hand: wheat germ, powdered, milk, and powdered buttermilk. Wheat germ is an easy way to add nutrition to your family's food. Sprinkle it over cereal or yogurt, or mix it into bread or other batters. To keep wheat germ fresh, store it in the refrigerator. Powdered milk can save a dash to the store "just for milk," and powdered buttermilk is convenient for baking several different dishes.

Pumpkin Bread

Ingredients:

3 c. sugar
1 c. vegetable oil
3 eggs
1 (15 oz.) can pumpkin
3 c. flour
½ tsp. salt

1 tsp. cloves
1 tsp. cinnamon
1 tsp. nutmeg
1 tsp. baking soda
½ tsp. baking powder

Directions:

1. Preheat oven to 350°.
2. Grease and flour a loaf pan.
3. Mix sugar, oil, and eggs. Add pumpkin.
4. Blend in flour, salt, cloves, cinnamon, nutmeg, baking soda, and baking powder.
5. Bake 45 minutes. Cool and remove from pan.

 Fill the sink half full of sudsy water and let your child "wash the dishes" while you cook. Supply him with funnels, utensils, and plastic containers of various sizes.

 Seen on a refrigerator magnet:

If you want to sit and visit, come anytime.
If you want to see my house, make an appointment!

Banana–Oatmeal Bread

Ingredients:

¼ c. vegetable shortening	2 tsp. baking powder
½ c. sugar	½ tsp. salt
2 eggs, beaten	½ tsp. baking soda
2 T. water	1 tsp. vanilla
1¾–2 c. mashed bananas	¾ c. regular or quick oats
1½ c. sifted flour	½ c. chopped nuts

Directions:

1. Preheat oven to 350°.
2. Cream shortening and sugar; add eggs.
3. Mix water with bananas.
4. Combine flour, baking powder, salt, and soda. Alternately add dry mixture and bananas to shortening mixture, blending well after each addition.
5. Add vanilla, oats, and nuts. Pour into a greased 8-cup loaf pan.
6. Let stand 30 minutes. Bake 50–60 minutes.

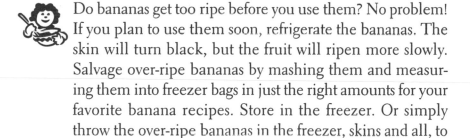 Do bananas get too ripe before you use them? No problem! If you plan to use them soon, refrigerate the bananas. The skin will turn black, but the fruit will ripen more slowly. Salvage over-ripe bananas by mashing them and measuring them into freezer bags in just the right amounts for your favorite banana recipes. Store in the freezer. Or simply throw the over-ripe bananas in the freezer, skins and all, to use for baking banana bread later.

Banana Nut Bread

Ingredients:

½ c. shortening
1 c. sugar
2 eggs, beaten
3 bananas, mashed
2 c. flour

1 tsp. baking soda
½ tsp. salt
2 T. milk
½ c. chopped nuts

Directions:

1. Preheat oven to 350°.
2. Cream together shortening and sugar; add eggs and bananas. Mix well. Add remaining ingredients except nuts and mix. Stir in nuts.
3. Bake in greased and floured loaf pan for 1 hour or until pick inserted in center comes out clean.
4. Cool 10–15 minutes and remove from pan. Can also be baked in muffin cups (approx. 25 minutes).

 Have a tea party with your children. Serve little sandwiches of banana bread spread with butter, peanut butter, or cream cheese. These make a great "on-the-go" breakfast, too.

 Why does everyone like bananas? Because they have appeal.

Quick, Easy Garlic Bread

Ingredients:

1 loaf unsliced French bread
1 tsp. garlic powder
¼ c. Parmesan cheese
½ c. soft butter
4 oz. cream cheese

Directions:

1. Mix all ingredients until smooth.
2. Spread over 2 sides of open-faced French bread. (There is enough for another half if you don't spread it too thick).
3. Broil until brown.
4. Slice.

 You can also try this spread with baked potatoes or on left-over mashed potatoes baked 20 minutes at 350.

 Baseball cap need washing? Form the cap over the bottom of an upside-down medium mixing bowl. Put the bowl and hat in the top rack of the dishwasher. Run the dishwasher load as usual. At the end of the cycle remove the hat and let it dry, still on the mixing bowl.

Refrigerator Bran Muffins

Ingredients:

1 c. boiling water	2½ tsp. soda
1 c. whole wheat bran	½ tsp. salt
1¾ c. sugar	1¾ c. buttermilk
½ c. vegetable shortening	2 c. All-Bran cereal
2 eggs	¾ c. golden raisins
2½ c. flour	

Directions:

1. Pour boiling water over the bran. Let stand until cool.
2. Cream sugar and shortening together. Add eggs, one at a time.
3. Sift dry ingredients and add alternately with buttermilk to mixture. Beat until smooth. Add cooled bran, All-Bran cereal, and raisins. Refrigerate overnight. Do not stir.
4. As needed, spoon batter into muffin tin, filling each muffin cup half full. Bake 20 minutes at 400°. Makes 3 dozen muffins. Batter keeps 2–3 weeks in refrigerator.

 The bran called for in this recipe is the actual bran you might find in a health food section. If you can't find this, 100% Bran cereal works just fine.

 Pop a batch of these yummy muffins in the oven when unexpected guests drop in for coffee.

 While this pie bakes, make a paper fan with your child to "cool" it when it comes out of the oven. You will need paper, crayons or markers, and tape. Let your child draw any type of picture or design, then make 1" folds, back and forth, in the paper. At one end, gather the folds together and tape to form a handle. Fan the pie until it is cool enough to eat.

Apple Walnut Muffins

Ingredients:

½ c. sugar
2 large apples, peeled and diced
2 eggs, lightly beaten
½ c. vegetable oil
2 tsp. vanilla
2 c. flour

2 tsp. baking soda
2 tsp. cinnamon
½ tsp. salt
¾ c. golden raisins
¾ c. walnuts, coarsely
chopped

Directions:

1. Preheat oven to 350°.
2. Combine sugar and apples in medium mixing bowl. Set aside.
3. Beat together eggs, oil, and vanilla. Add to apples.
4. In a separate bowl combine remaining ingredients, mixing well. Stir into apple mixture; combine thoroughly. Batter will be stiff.
5. Spoon into greased muffin cups. Bake 25 minutes or until toothpick inserted in center comes out clean. Makes 18 muffins.

 Fill a glass half full of water. Add 1–2 tablespoons of oil to the glass. Observe with your child how the oil sits on top of the water; they don't blend together. Now stir the water and watch what happens. Add food coloring to the oil to help you see how the oil and water do not mix.

 Treat your family to the golden raisins used in this recipe instead of the usual "purple" ones. Little helpers can snack on this new tasty treat!

Chocolate Chip Muffins

Ingredients:

1 ½ c. flour
½ c. sugar
3 tsp. baking powder
¼ tsp. salt

1 c. chocolate chips
1 egg
1 c. milk
⅓ c. butter (5 ⅓ T.)

Directions:

1. Preheat oven to 375°.
2. Mix dry ingredients. Add chocolate chips.
3. In microwave, melt butter in Pyrex measuring cup. Cool. Add egg and milk. Mix ingredients, but do not beat.
4. Stir into flour mixture.
5. Pour into greased or paper-lined muffin tins. Bake 20–25 minutes. Makes 12 muffins.

 Try mini-chocolate chips in this recipe.

 Half the fun of baking with chocolate chips are the stolen morsels. Since you only need 1 cup of chips, don't patrol too carefully what happens to the rest.

Feather–Light Muffins

Ingredients:

⅓ c. shortening
½ c. sugar
1 egg
1½ c. cake flour
1½ tsp. baking powder
½ tsp. salt
¼ tsp. nutmeg
½ c. milk

Topping:
½ c. sugar
1 tsp. ground cinnamon
¼ c. butter or margarine, melted

Directions:

1. Preheat oven to 325°.
2. In a mixing bowl cream shortening, sugar, and egg.
3. Combine dry ingredients; add to creamed mixture alternately with milk.
4. Fill greased muffin tins ⅔ full. Bake 20–25 minutes or until golden.
5. Let cool for 3–4 minutes. Meanwhile, combine sugar and cinnamon in a small bowl. Dip the top of each muffin in melted butter, then in sugar mixture. Serve warm. Makes 8–10 muffins.

 Cake flour adds a tender texture to baked goods. If you don't have cake flour, try this: For each ½ c. of cake flour called for, substitute 1 T. cornstarch, then fill up to ½-cup line with flour.

 When preparing muffins, keep mixing to a minimum: 10–20 seconds of stirring will do. Ignore remaining lumps. If you overmix, the gluten in the flour will toughen the dough.

 Taste and see that the LORD is good; happy are those who take refuge in him (Psalm 34:8 NRSV).

Carrot–Pineapple Muffins (or Cake)

Ingredients:

1 c. vegetable oil	2 tsp. baking soda
1 c. sugar	1 tsp. salt
3 eggs	2 c. peeled, shredded carrots
1 tsp. vanilla	1 c. shredded coconut
2 c. flour	1 c. chopped nuts
1½ tsp. cinnamon	1 c. crushed pineapple

Directions:

1. Preheat oven to 350°.
2. Mix and blend oil, sugar, eggs, and vanilla.
3. Sift dry ingredients and add to first mixture.
4. Blend in carrots, coconut, nuts, and pineapple.
5. Treat pan with nonstick spray. Bake 20–25 minutes for muffins or 45 minutes for cake. Makes 2 dozen muffins or a 9" x 12" cake.

 If you don't use every muffin cup, fill the empty ones with water. This keeps the pan from scorching and also adds moisture to the oven.

Zucchini Muffins

Ingredients:

4 c. flour	¾ c. oil
1 tsp. salt	¾ c. applesauce
1 tsp. baking soda	3 c. grated zucchini
1½ tsp. baking powder	1 c. chopped nuts
3 tsp. cinnamon	1½ c. raisins
4 eggs	1 tsp. vanilla
2 c. sugar	

Directions:

1. Preheat oven to 350°.
2. Mix flour, salt, baking soda, baking powder, and cinnamon. Set aside.
3. In another bowl mix together remaining ingredients. Add flour mixture and stir until well mixed.
4. Bake in paper-lined muffin cups for 25–30 minutes. Makes 3 dozen muffins.

 These muffins are good anytime of the day, not just for breakfast. Instead of using zucchini, try apples or bananas — whichever you have on hand. Muffins can be baked ahead and frozen in freezer bags. Remove the number you need and thaw at room temperature or microwave for 15–30 seconds.

Blueberry Muffins

Ingredients:

¼ c. butter, melted
⅔ c. sugar
1 egg
¾ c. milk
¼ tsp. salt
¾ tsp. baking soda
2 c. flour
¾ c. frozen blueberries

Directions:

1. Preheat oven to 400°.
2. Mix all ingredients except blueberries.
3. Gently stir in blueberries. Spoon into muffin pans.
4. Bake 20–25 minutes. Makes 12 muffins.

 When fresh blueberries are in season in early summer, watch for the initially high price to go down before buying some pints. Rinse the blueberries in a colander, sorting out any green ones and pulling off woody stems. Drain well and freeze in a single layer on a cookie sheet. When frozen, transfer the blueberries to freezer bags for use as needed in blueberry pancakes, muffins, fruit salad, or granola.

Hot Cross Muffins

Ingredients:

1⅔ c. flour

⅔ c. sugar

2 tsp. baking powder

¾ tsp. cinnamon

½ tsp. salt

1 egg

⅓ c. vegetable oil

⅔ cup evaporated milk (or regular milk)

¾ c. raisins

Topping:

⅓ c. powdered sugar

1½ tsp. evaporated milk
    (or regular milk)

Directions:

1. Preheat oven to 400°.
2. Sift together flour, sugar, baking powder, cinnamon, and salt. Make a well in center of the mixture.
3. Beat together egg, oil, and ⅔ cup evaporated milk. Pour gently into the well. Stir in raisins.
4. Spoon dough into greased muffin tins, filling cups ⅔ full. Bake 20 minutes.
5. Remove muffins from tins and cool 5 minutes. Combine powdered sugar and remaining milk into a glaze and drizzle over top of each muffin, forming a cross. Makes 12 muffins.

 With a spoon or clean paintbrush, let your child "paint" the glaze in the shape of a cross on each muffin. Talk about how the cross is special to Christians because long ago on a cross Jesus showed how much he loves us.

 Take these for coffee after an Easter sunrise service.

Johnny Appleseed Pizza

Ingredients:

2 T. flour

½ c. brown sugar

½ c. white sugar

1 T. cinnamon

1 loaf frozen bread dough, thawed

2 c. shredded cheddar cheese

5 c. apples, sliced

⅓ cup margarine or butter

Directions:

1. Preheat oven to 350°.
2. Mix flour, sugars, and cinnamon. Set aside.
3. Spread dough on greased cookie sheet.
4. Sprinkle dough with cheese.
5. Put apples on top.
6. Sprinkle with sugar mix. Dot with margarine.
7. Bake 20–30 minutes. Serves 15.

 Children can easily spread cheese on dough, arrange apples, and sprinkle sugar over all.

 Talk about the story of Johnny Appleseed with your child. You can probably find a good book at the library about this interesting historical figure.

 Johnny Appleseed's Prayer

The Lord is good to me,
And so I thank the Lord,
Who giveth me
The things I need
The sun and the rain
And the appleseed . . .
   (you can add your own thankfulness here)
The Lord is good to me.

Scones with Devonshire Cream

Ingredients:

1½ c. flour
¼ c. sugar
¼ tsp. salt
1½ tsp. baking powder
¼ c. margarine or butter, cold
⅓ cup raisins, dried cranberries,
    currants, or chopped nuts (opt.)
1 egg
2 T. milk

Devonshire Cream:
1 (8 oz.) pkg. cream cheese,
    softened
⅓ c. dairy sour cream
2 T. sugar

Directions:

1. Preheat oven to 425°.
2. Mix dry ingredients. Cut in margarine. Add raisins or nuts. Add egg and milk and mix with fork.
3. Roll ½" thick, adding only enough flour to prevent sticking. Cut with 2" round cutter.
4. Bake 2" apart on greased baking sheet for 12–15 minutes. Makes at least 12, depending on how you cut the dough.
5. While scones are baking, mix together ingredients for Devonshire Cream until smooth and light. Refrigerate until serving.
6. Cool scones. Serve with Devonshire Cream.

 To "cut in" butter or margarine, use two knives, pulling them past each other in opposite directions with a cutting motion, until the mixture resembles small peas. Or you can add very cold butter, cut into chunks, to the dry ingredients in a food processor. Mix, using quick, short bursts, to lightly blend the butter with the flour. Don't overmix. The mixture should resemble crumbs or grains.

Monkey Bread

Ingredients:

2 (1 lb.) loaves frozen bread dough, thawed
1 c. brown sugar, firmly packed
½ c. butter or margarine
2 small (3.5 oz.) boxed vanilla or butterscotch pudding
   (Cook & Serve, not instant)
1½ tsp. cinnamon
2 T. milk
1 c. walnuts or pecans

Directions:

1. Spray 9" x 13" pan with nonstick spray. Tear pieces of one loaf of bread and scatter in pan.
2. Mix next 5 ingredients together and cook over low heat, until margarine is melted. Cool and pour half of mixture over layer of bread pieces.
3. Add pieces of second loaf of bread and pour rest of mixture over all. Let bread rise to top of pan. Preheat oven to 350°.
4. Sprinkle with nuts and bake 30 minutes.

 Older children can help cut the bread into quarters with kitchen shears. Talk about halves and quarters and other fractions.

 You can prepare this the night before by using frozen bread rolls instead of the thawed loaves. Follow the recipe, using the frozen rolls. Cover the pan with a cloth and let it rise in the refrigerator overnight. In the morning, the dough should be doubled in size and ready to bake.

One day a distracted mommy unplugged her chest freezer so she could plug in a glue gun. Of course, she forgot to plug the freezer back in, and later when she removed some vegetables from the freezer and rearranged its bulging contents, she forgot to close the lid.

Several hours later she passed the freezer and balloons of frozen bread dough caught her eye. It had thawed and was rising above the chest. Her family enjoyed many, many rolls in the days to come.

Monkey Cinnamon Bread

Ingredients:

3 cans buttermilk biscuits
¾ c. sugar
1 T. cinnamon

½ c. butter
1 c. brown sugar
¼ tsp. vanilla

Directions:

1. Preheat oven to 350°.
2. Cut biscuits into quarters. Combine sugar and cinnamon in a small plastic bag. Shake each biscuit piece in the bag with the cinnamon and sugar until coated.
3. Spray bundt pan or 9" x 13" dish with nonstick spray. Arrange biscuits around in pan.
4. Cook butter with brown sugar on medium heat until it bubbles, stirring often to avoid burning; add vanilla. Pour evenly over biscuits and bake 25 minutes.

 Let the children help you shake the biscuits in the sugar mixture and arrange the pieces of bread in the pan.

 Warning! Don't use a pan with a loose bottom (springform) for this type of recipe, or you will have butter and sugar oozing all over your oven.

If something catches fire in your oven or on the stove ... don't panic! Calmly reach for the baking soda or salt (which you have wisely placed in the cabinet nearby for just this moment) and pour the contents onto the fire. No matter how tempting it is, DO NOT use water or liquid on a kitchen fire.

 While you are cooking, talk with your children about how to handle a crisis, how soda smothers the fire, and about other fire safety rules.

Scandinavian Almond Coffee Cake

Ingredients:

Part 1:

½ c. butter or margarine,
  softened
1 c. flour
2 T. water

Part 2:

½ cup butter or margarine
1 c. water
1 tsp. almond extract
1 c. flour
3 eggs

Glaze:

1½ c. powdered sugar
2 T. softened butter
1–1½ tsp. almond extract
1–2 tsp. water
sliced almonds

Directions:

1. Preheat oven to 350°.
2. Cut ½ cup softened butter into flour. Sprinkle 2 tablespoons water over mixture. Mix with fork. Round into ball; divide in half. Can be mixed in food processor.
3. On ungreased baking sheet pat each half into a strip (12" x 3"). Place strips about 3" apart. This step can be completed the night before. If you do, cover dough and refrigerate.
4. In a medium saucepan heat ½ cup butter and 1 cup water to rolling boil. Remove from heat. Quickly stir in almond extract, flour, and eggs, one at a time, stirring vigorously over low heat until mixture forms ball (about 1 minute). Remove from heat.
5. Divide in half; spread each half evenly over strips, covering completely.
6. Bake 60 minutes or until top is crisp and brown; cool.
7. Mix together glaze ingredients.
8. Frost with glaze; sprinkle gently with nuts.
9. To serve, cut into diagonal strips. Serves 10–12.

Step 1 can be done in a food processor. Mix until dough forms a ball in bowl. To save yourself time, you can do steps 1 and 2, cover and refrigerate, and start at step 3 in the morning.

 Be sure your children scc this coffee cake go into the oven. The cream puff topping looks odd before baking, but puffy, light, and golden brown afterward!

Raspberry Cream Cheese Coffee Cake

Ingredients:

2¼ c. flour
¾ c. sugar
¾ c. butter
½ tsp. baking powder
½ tsp. baking soda
¼ tsp. salt
¾ c. sour cream
1 egg
1 tsp. almond extract

Topping:
1 (8 oz.) pkg. cream cheese, softened
¼ c. sugar
1 egg
½ c. raspberry preserves
½ c. sliced almonds

Directions:

1. Preheat oven to 350°.
2. Grease and flour bottom and sides of 9" or 10" springform pan. Combine flour and ¾ c. sugar. Cut in butter until mixture resembles coarse crumbs. Reserve 1 c. crumb mixture. Set aside.
3. To remaining crumb mixture, add baking powder, baking soda, salt, sour cream, 1 egg, and almond extract; blend well. Spread batter over bottom and 2" up sides of prepared pan. (Batter should be about 3" thick on sides.)
4. In small bowl, combine cream cheese, ¼ cup sugar, and 1 egg; blend well. Pour over batter in pan.
5. Carefully spoon preserves evenly over cheese filling.
6. In small bowl combine 1 cup reserved crumb mixture and sliced almonds. Sprinkle over top.
7. Bake 45–55 minutes or until filling is set and crust is deep golden brown. Cool 15 minutes. Remove sides of pan. Cut into wedges; serve warm or cool. Refrigerate leftovers. Serves 16.

 A springform pan is a wonderful invention! This round pan with separate bottom and sides clamps shut to keep the batter in, and "springs" open to allow easy removal of the finished cake. Use for cheesecakes, this coffee cake, or other thick batters. Don't use for thin batters, as the batter will ooze out and create havoc in your oven.

 This beautiful coffee cake will bring raves at women's meetings or for brunch on Christmas morning. It is more involved to make, however. If taking it to a morning gathering, prepare this the night before.

Apple Coffee Cake

Ingredients:

1 c. vegetable oil	1 tsp. salt
2 eggs	1 tsp. cinnamon
2 c. sugar	1 tsp. soda
3 c. flour	3 c. apples, peeled and diced
1 tsp. vanilla	1 c. pecans, chopped

Directions:

1. Preheat oven to 350°.
2. Mix and bake in ungreased 9" x 13" pan for 45 minutes. Serves 9.

The beds are all made and the dishes are done.
The kids are all shiny and ready for fun;
The clothes are all ironed, no dirt on this floor.
No doubt you've guessed I'm calling next door.
— Anonymous

. . . When you visit next door, this cake might be a nice gift to take along!

Here's a good game for waiting at the table in a restaurant: Using 3 little cream containers, place a penny under one of them, and ask your child to keep watching to see where the penny ends up as you move the containers around.

Sunday Special Coffee Cake

Ingredients:

1 ½ c. flour
2 ½ tsp. baking powder
½ tsp. salt
1 egg
¾ c. sugar
⅓ c. butter, melted
½ c. milk
1 tsp. vanilla

Topping:
½ c. sugar
¼ c. flour
¼ c. butter, softened
1 tsp. cinnamon

Directions:

1. Preheat oven to 375°.
2. Grease 8" square or 9" round pan. Combine ingredients for topping in bowl and mix until crumbly. Set aside.
3. Sift flour with baking powder and salt. Set aside.
4. In medium bowl beat egg until frothy. Add sugar and butter; then add milk and vanilla.
5. Beat in flour mixture with wooden spoon.
6. Pour into pan. Sprinkle evenly with topping and bake 25–30 minutes. Serve warm. Serves 9.

 I have never seen the righteous forsaken or their children begging bread (Psalm 37:25).

 When your child is sick, serve her meal on a tray set with a pretty napkin and china dishes. Turn on a tape of soothing music.

Cream Cheese Crescent Danish

Ingredients:

2 (8 oz.) cans crescent dinner rolls
2 (8 oz.) pkgs. cream cheese
1 c. sugar, divided
1 tsp. vanilla
1 egg, separated
½ c. chopped walnuts

Directions:

1. Preheat oven to 350°.
2. Grease 9" x 13" pan. Spread out 1 pkg. of rolls on bottom of pan, pinching together seams to make a smooth layer of dough.
3. Beat cream cheese, ¾ cup sugar, and vanilla until creamy. Spread over the dough in pan. Spread second package of rolls on top.
4. Beat egg white until frothy. Spread on top with brush. Sprinkle with remaining ¼ cup sugar and nuts.
5. Bake 30–35 minutes. Cool completely. Cut and refrigerate leftovers. Serves 12.

 Beating egg whites is probably not your favorite pastime, so try these hints to help ensure success: Clear egg whites entirely of yolk, because the slightest fat from the yolk will lessen the volume of the whites. The bowl and beaters you use should be thoroughly clean as well. Choose a deep bowl that is neither aluminum (which will gray the eggs) nor plastic (which frequently contains a chemical which deters volume development).

Beaten egg whites should be stiff (hold a peak when you pull out the beaters), but not dry.

Fold beaten egg whites into a heavier mixture gently, by hand, to retain as much air in the whites as possible.

Family Pancakes

Ingredients:

2 eggs
1 c. sour cream
2 c. milk
2½ c. Bisquick
2 T. butter, melted
½ tsp. vanilla

Directions:

1. Beat eggs in a large bowl. Blend in sour cream. Stir in milk.
2. Add Bisquick and beat with wire whisk just until smooth. Stir in melted butter and vanilla.
3. Cook pancakes on large griddle until lightly golden and done in the center.
4. Serve with your favorite syrups or jam. Makes 20 4" pancakes.

 This is such a simple batter to mix, kids will be able to help with the measuring, stirring, cooking, and certainly the eating!

Puffed Pancake

Ingredients:

¼ c. margarine or butter
3 eggs
¾ c. milk
¾ c. flour

Directions:

1. Preheat oven to 425°.
2. In oven-proof, 3-quart round casserole dish, melt margarine in oven.
3. Whir eggs in blender on high for 1 minute. Slowly add milk and flour to eggs, whirring 30 seconds after each addition.
4. Pour mixture over melted margarine.
5. Bake 20–25 minutes until puffy and brown. Pancake will rise above pan.
6. Dump pancake upside down out of casserole dish onto plate. Sprinkle with powdered sugar and fresh lemon juice. Serves 4–6.

 Turn on the oven light and let the children watch the pancake puff. When the oven timer signals 20 minutes, shout "Pancake Alert!" and dump the pancake onto a plate so the kids can watch it deflate.

 An English Prayer

For rosy apples, juicy plums,
And yellow pears so sweet,
For hips and haws and bush and hedge,
And flowers at our feet,
For ears of corn all ripe and dry,
And colored leaves on trees,
We thank you, Heavenly Father God,
For such good gifts as these.
      —Author unknown

Grandma's French Toast

Ingredients:

1 stick (½ c.) butter, melted
⅓ c. brown sugar, packed
1–2 tsp. cinnamon
4 eggs
2 c. milk
⅔ loaf French bread

Directions:

1. Preheat oven to 350°.
2. In warming oven melt butter in a 9" x 13" baking pan; watch that it doesn't burn.
3. Mix brown sugar and cinnamon; sprinkle over butter.
4. Mix eggs and milk.
5. Cut bread (if it isn't already sliced) into ¾" slices. Dip slices into egg mixture and lay in pan. Pour any extra egg mixture on top.
6. Bake 20–30 minutes or until top is golden brown. Loosen from pan and serve immediately to prevent sticking. Serves 6.

 Prepare this recipe up to baking the night before and refrigerate it. Imagine this easy way to have French Toast on Christmas morning! All you will need to add is a mug of creamy hot chocolate or spiced tea for a memorable breakfast.

Enchurritos

Ingredients:

1 doz. flour tortillas
1 (28 oz.) can mild enchilada sauce
1 lb. cooked meat (chicken, ground beef, or sausage)
1 lb. shredded cheddar cheese

Directions:

1. Preheat oven to 375°.
2. Warm enchilada sauce in small saucepan and remove from heat.
3. Dip warm tortillas in enchilada sauce; put on plate and fill with meat and a pinch of cheese.
4. Roll burrito-style (fold two sides in and roll up, bottom to top). Repeat with remaining tortillas, arranging them in an ungreased baking dish. Pour remaining enchilada sauce over the enchurritos and top with remaining cheese.
5. Bake 15–20 minutes. Serves 8.

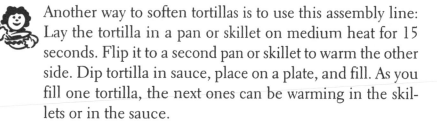 Another way to soften tortillas is to use this assembly line: Lay the tortilla in a pan or skillet on medium heat for 15 seconds. Flip it to a second pan or skillet to warm the other side. Dip tortilla in sauce, place on a plate, and fill. As you fill one tortilla, the next ones can be warming in the skillets or in the sauce.

Buffet Eggs

Ingredients:

4 T. butter, divided
2 T. all-purpose flour
1 c. sour cream
2 doz. eggs

¾ tsp. salt
⅛ tsp. white pepper
chopped parsley

Directions:

1. In a small pan, melt 2 tablespoons butter on medium heat. Stir in flour and cook until bubbly. Remove pan from heat and blend in sour cream.
2. Return pan to heat and cook until bubbly and smooth. Set aside.
3. Mix eggs, salt, and pepper together.
4. In a large frying pan, over medium heat, melt the remaining 2 tablespoons butter. Pour in eggs and cook, gently lifting the cooked portion to allow the uncooked eggs to flow underneath, until eggs are softly set.
5. Remove from heat and gently stir in sour cream mixture.
6. Turn eggs into a serving dish and garnish with parsley. Keep warm on electric serving tray for up to an hour. You could keep the eggs warm using a crockpot on low setting as well. Serves 12.
7. Optional: If desired, prepare a variety of condiments for toppings. Try 1 cup each of: crisp bacon bits, cooked sausage crumbles, shredded Swiss or cheddar cheese, sliced ripe olives, sliced green onion, chopped red onion, salmon shreds, small cooked shrimp, sour cream, salsa, chopped fresh tomatoes.

 This is a great way to serve eggs to a large group. The eggs will keep beautifully and can be garnished according to each person's tastes. For a heartier meal, serve baked potato "boats" to hold the eggs.

Cheese Bacon Crescent Squares

Ingredients:

1 (8 oz.) can Pillsbury refrigerated quick crescent dinner rolls
¾ c. (3 oz.) shredded Swiss cheese
¾ c. (3 oz.) shredded mozzarella or Monterey Jack cheese
1 egg, beaten
¼ c. chopped fresh onion
¾ c. milk
¼–½ c. sliced, stuffed green olives (opt.)
1 (4 oz.) can mushroom stems and pieces, drained
6 slices bacon, fried, drained, and crumbled
1 T. minced parsley (opt.)

Directions:

1. Preheat oven to 375°.
2. Press crescent dough onto bottom and 2" up sides of 9" x 13" pan to form crust, sealing perforations. Sprinkle cheeses over dough.
3. Combine egg, onion, milk, olives, and mushrooms. Pour over cheeses. Sprinkle with bacon and parsley.
4. Bake 22–28 minutes or until crust is deep golden brown and filling is set. Cool 5 minutes before cutting into squares. Serves 4–6.

To prepare bacon with less mess and less remaining fat, use the microwave. Stack up to 6 strips of bacon at a time in a baking dish between 2 layers of paper towels, 3 strips to a layer. Watch carefully that it doesn't burn. Approximate cooking time: 1 minute per bacon strip.

If your children search for and pick out any bits of onion in a dish, try the equivalent amount of dry minced onion instead of fresh onion. For this recipe, 1 T. dry minced onion equals ¼ c. fresh onion.

Brunch Casserole

Ingredients:

1 lb. bulk sausage (sweet, Italian, or turkey) or ¾ lb. ham, cubed
6 slices bread (white or wheat)
½ lb. sharp cheddar cheese, grated
5 eggs
pinch of salt
¾ tsp. dry mustard
2½ c. milk
1 (10½ oz.) can cream of celery soup

Directions:

1. Brown and drain sausage. Tear or cut bread into cubes. Beat eggs and add a little salt.
2. Spray or grease a 9" x 13" baking dish. Place bread cubes in the bottom of the pan. Add sausage and grated cheese.
3. Blend eggs, salt, dry mustard, milk, and soup. Pour over bread, sausage, and cheese.
4. Cover and refrigerate overnight.
5. Bake in preheated 300° oven for 1 hour or until set. Serves 8.

 Stretch your meal boundaries and enjoy this for dinner with a green salad and frozen fruit bars for dessert.

 Family Prayer

Lord, behold our family here assembled,
We thank you for this place in which we dwell,
for the love that unites us,
for the peace accorded us this day,
for the hope with which we expect the morrow;
for the health, the work, the food, the bright skies
That make our lives delightful;
For our friends in all parts of the earth.
Amen.

      — Robert Louis Stevenson

Breakfast Frittata

Ingredients:

8 slices bread (remove crust)
½ lb. (approx.) cooked,
    cubed ham; cooked,
    crumbled bacon; or sliced
    Little Smokies
¼ c. minced onion
1 (4 oz.) can chopped green
    chilies

4 c. (16 oz.) Monterey Jack
    cheese, grated
2 c. milk
½ tsp. dry mustard
½ tsp. oregano
½ tsp. garlic powder
¼ tsp. salt
¼ tsp. pepper
10 eggs

Directions:

1. Preheat oven to 350°.
2. Lightly grease 9" x 13" baking dish. Layer bread slices, meat, minced onion, chilies, and cheese in dish.
3. Mix milk with spices and eggs and pour over cheese.
4. Cover; refrigerate overnight.
5. Bake uncovered for 1 hour. Serves 8.

 For a late morning brunch serve with a basket of corn muffins and fresh melon slices.

 Egg cartons have many uses "after eggs." Cut the cups apart and create an instant tea set (best used with pretend tea). Turn one cup into a hat for a doll. Turn upside down and decorate to become a tiny village. See what else you can create!

Frozen Fruit Cup

Ingredients:

1 (16 oz.) pkg. frozen strawberries in syrup, thawed
1 (20 oz.) can crushed pineapple with juice
2½ c. canned apricots, diced
4 diced bananas
2 c. fruit juice

Directions:

1. Mix and freeze in muffin tins.
2. After at least 24 hours, pop frozen fruit out of muffin tins. Store in plastic bags in freezer.

 Keep fruit in the freezer and ready to serve! Half an hour before serving, place each portion in a small clear bowl or those goblets you never get to use.

 Place a collection of different-sized objects in a large bowl. Have your child move the items into another container using kitchen tongs. This will help develop small motor skills.

Caramelized Bacon

Ingredients:

½ lb. bacon strips
⅛ c. prepared mustard (approx.)
⅛ c. brown sugar (approx.)

Directions:

1. Preheat oven to 400°.
2. Separate bacon strips and place on baking sheet with sides, or better yet, on a broiler pan with slits in the top. Spread each slice with mustard; sprinkle brown sugar on top.
3. Bake 10 minutes. Watch so that it doesn't burn. Serves 4.

 Add this pizzazz to a weekend brunch. Serve it with Grandma's French Toast or Family Pancakes.

 Use tongs for turning bacon, chicken, or pork chops.

 If you have two or three strips of Carmelized Bacon left over, use them in a spinach salad: Combine fresh spinach leaves (rinsed, dried, and torn), crumbled Carmelized Bacon strips, and a diced, hard-boiled egg. Top with Caesar salad dressing.

Sausage Swirls

Ingredients:

4 c. flour
¼ c. cornmeal
2 T. sugar
2 tsp. baking powder
1 tsp. salt
⅔ c. vegetable oil
¾–1 c. milk
2 lb. uncooked bulk pork sausage

Directions:

1. Preheat oven to 400°.
2. Combine flour, cornmeal, sugar, baking powder, and salt. Stir in oil until mixture resembles coarse crumbs. Gradually stir in enough milk to form a soft dough.
3. Turn onto floured board; knead lightly for 30 seconds. Roll into two 16" x 10" rectangles.
4. Crumble uncooked sausage over dough to within 2" of all sides. Carefully roll up from 16" end. Wrap in foil; chill 1 hour or overnight.
5. Cut into 2" slices. Bake 15–20 minutes, or until brown. Serve warm or cold. Makes about 4 dozen.

The pork sausage will cook in the oven as these rolls bake. The pan should have sides to prevent grease from dripping off of pan.

Slice a peeled banana into circles about ½" thick. Dip slices into orange or pineapple juice to prevent browning and place them in the freezer on a cookie sheet until they are frozen solid. Then transfer them to a zip-closure bag in the freezer to keep for a quick snack.

Beyond Boring Breakfasts!

*W*ho says breakfast has to be a bowl of cereal, an egg, or a quickly gulped glass of milk or juice? How about pizza? How about a bowl of hot rice with butter, cinnamon, sugar, and a little milk poured over it all? Delicious! Be brave, be daring, wake up your family with surprises at breakfast. Here are a few ideas to get you going. Be creative and you'll soon discover your own favorites.

- Cover a slice of bread with a piece of cheese and toast in a toaster oven or under the broiler. Top with fresh apple slices and sprinkle lightly with cinnamon.
- Toast an English muffin half. Place a slice of ham on muffin, spread with cream cheese or cottage cheese, and top it all off with sliced strawberries.
- Place sliced chicken, turkey, or ham on one piece of white or raisin bread toast. Cover with fresh or mandarin orange slices or peach slices. Spread with vanilla-flavored yogurt. Top with another piece of toast for a yummy sandwich.
- Try crisp bacon and sliced banana on toast spread with peanut butter and fruit jam.
- Toast English muffins and spread with spaghetti sauce, cooked sausage, and cheese. Broil until cheese is melted.
- Enjoy a mug of cream of tomato soup and whole wheat toast fingers.
- Slice off the top of an apple. Hollow out the core, leaving bottom intact. Brush hollow with citrus juice (lemon, orange, pineapple). Fill with peanut butter mixed with raisins, or cream cheese mixed with fruit and nuts. Replace top. This is a good "on-the-go" treat. For young children, cut the apple into slices and have them "dip" the filling.
- Make sandwiches from banana bread. Spread with cream cheese, peanut butter, or jelly.

Oasis of

BEVERAGES, APPETIZERS, AND SNACKS

White Hot Chocolate

Ingredients:

3 c. half and half, divided
⅔ c. white chocolate baking chips
1 cinnamon stick (3")
⅛ tsp. ground nutmeg
1 tsp. vanilla
¼ tsp. almond extract

Directions:

1. In a saucepan combine ¼ cup half and half, white chocolate chips, cinnamon stick, and nutmeg. Stir over low heat until chips are melted; discard cinnamon stick.
2. Add remaining half and half; stir until heated through.
3. Remove from heat; add vanilla and almond extract. Sprinkle with cinnamon, if desired. Serves 4.

 Freshly ground nutmeg is easy to have on hand. Whole nutmeg can be grated on the smallest side of a hand grater or in a special spice mill. Fresh nutmeg adds flavor to cookies, fruit dishes, and vegetables such as carrots, potatoes, and spinach.

Cappuccino

Ingredients:

1 c. coffee creamer
1 c. instant chocolate drink (Quik)
⅔ c. instant coffee crystals
½ c. sugar
½ tsp. cinnamon
¼ tsp. nutmeg

Directions:

1. Mix ingredients together and store in airtight container.
2. To serve, add 3 tablespoons mixture (more or less to your liking) to 8 ounces of hot water.

 One mom's definition of "comfort food": hot tea or cocoa in my favorite mug (but it's just not the same if I'm not in my old flannel bathrobe).

 Offering and preparing a beverage for a family member or friend is a warm, gracious gesture that says "Welcome." Keep a variety of beverages on hand to satisfy the slightest thirst.

 Make it a ritual to prepare a warm, fragrant beverage for yourself or family after an especially hard day.

Hot Sunny Cider

Ingredients:

1 qt. apple cider (or apple juice)
1 c. orange juice
1 c. pineapple juice
1 tsp. whole allspice
1 tsp. whole cloves
2 cinnamon sticks (2" long)

Directions:

1. In saucepan combine all ingredients. Simmer 10–15 minutes.
2. Strain and serve. This can be easily doubled and served from a crockpot. Serves 6–8.

 'Tis a gift to be simple,
'Tis a gift to be free,
'Tis a gift to come down
where we ought to be,
And when we find ourselves
in the place just right,
'Twill be in the valley
of love and delight.
— Shaker hymn

Cranberry Cider

Ingredients:

2 qts. apple cider (or apple juice)
1½ qts. cranberry juice
¼ c. brown sugar
1 tea ball of whole cloves
1 orange, sliced in pinwheels
4 cinnamon sticks (about 3" long)

Directions:

1. Combine first four ingredients in a crockpot.
2. Simmer at least 2 hours.
3. Serve with a garnish of orange slice or cinnamon stick. Serves 12.

 Enjoy this fragrant drink on a rainy afternoon with a gathering of good friends.

 You can use a tea ball to hold the small spices. Then you won't have to strain the cider. If you don't have a tea ball, use a coffee filter tied closed with twine.

Spiced Tea

Ingredients:

1 ½ c. Tang
¾ c. sugar
1 ½ c. sweetened lemon instant tea (powdered)
2 tsp. cinnamon
2 tsp. cloves

Directions:

Mix well. Use 1–2 teaspoons for each cup of boiling water.

 This fragrant, comforting tea is a good gift to send to college students, to take on vacation, or to take to new moms.

 When your children are ill with stomach flu, fight diarrhea with the BRAT meal: bananas, rice, applesauce, and toast. If they are having problems keeping food down, try tea or ginger ale (of course, check with your doctor first).

"Mock" Orange Julius

Ingredients:

1 (12 oz.) can frozen orange juice concentrate
2 c. milk
2 c. water
¼ to ½ c. granulated sugar
½ tsp. vanilla
20–24 ice cubes

Directions:

1. Put all ingredients into blender in two batches. Blend for one minute or until ice is blended fine.
2. Serve at once. Serves 6.

 With your supervision, let children push the blender buttons and watch the blender whip its magic with the ice cubes.

 While making a blender-full of chocolate shakes for my family, the base of the blender container came unscrewed. When I lifted the container, chocolate shake poured out onto the counter. It ran under every appliance, gushed down the crack between the stove and cupboard, and spread across the floor.

Candy Nog Punch

Ingredients:

1 c. whipping cream
1 qt. peppermint ice cream
2 c. eggnog
1 pt. and 12 oz. club soda
red food coloring
⅓ c. crushed peppermint candy
16 peppermint sticks

Directions:

1. Whip whipping cream until it holds soft peaks; set aside.
2. Add eggnog and soda to ice cream in punch bowl. Mix. Stir in a few drops of food coloring.
3. Spoon whipped cream over mixture and sprinkle with crushed peppermint candy. Place peppermint stick in each cup. Serves 16.

 Here is a festive punch for a Christmas gathering.

 Remember those for whom the season may be lonely.

For I was hungry and you gave me something to eat, I was thirsty and you gave me something to drink, I was a stranger and you invited me in (Matthew 25:35).

Holiday Punch

Ingredients:

1 (12 oz.) can frozen orange juice concentrate
¾ c. sugar
1 qt. water
1 (6 oz.) pkg. tropical punch Kool Aid
1 (46 oz.) can pineapple juice
2 liters Sprite

Directions:

1. Mix up orange juice according to package directions.
2. Add sugar and water to package of Kool Aid.
3. Chill mixture until ready to use.
4. Add pineapple juice and Sprite to punch mixture. (May make frozen ring of part of one bottle of Sprite to keep punch cold.) Makes 24 cups.

 My two- and three-year-old daughters always make Kool Aid. One day I was distracted by a phone call and didn't realize an argument had broken out over stirring. The Kool Aid didn't just spill; it hit the ceiling and came down like a fountain, covering cupboards, counters, and kids. My floors are still sticky!

Poco Pepper Snacks

Ingredients:

1 can Pillsbury crescent rolls
6 oz. cream cheese
1–2 T. diced green chilies
dash onion powder or onion salt
5–7 drops Tabasco Sauce
⅓ c. cheddar cheese, shredded

Directions:

1. Preheat oven to 375°.
2. Pinch two triangles of crescent dough together to make a rectangle; make 4 rectangles.
3. Mix remaining ingredients together. Spread ¼ of mix on each rectangle.
4. Roll up dough; pinch closed and slice into ¾" circles.
5. Place circles onto ungreased cookie sheet.
6. Bake about 15 minutes until golden brown. Makes 20.

 Poco is the Spanish word for "little." These little snacks are spicy.

 It takes time and energy to cook with your child. Be sure you're in the frame of mind to work slowly, with mess. Treat cooking as a special time together.

 I once made potato salad and used cayenne pepper for garnishment by mistake instead of paprika. It was a smashing success!

Cheese Crispies

Ingredients:

2 sticks (½ lb.) butter
2 c. flour
½ tsp. salt
½ lb. (2 c.) sharp cheddar cheese, grated
dash cayenne pepper
2 c. Rice Krispies

Directions:

1. Preheat oven to 325°.
2. Mix first five ingredients well with hands, blender, or mixer. Add Rice Krispies by hand.
3. Roll mixture into small balls the size of marbles.
4. Cook on lightly greased cookie sheet for 12–15 minutes.
5. Sprinkle with paprika and store in covered container. Makes approximately 170.

 Put the mixture in the microwave a few seconds to soften it so you can more easily roll it into balls.

 This dish is tailor-made for little hands. Let children help mix and roll small balls.

 Start good habits early. Hands should be washed 15–20 seconds in soapy water before handling food. Long hair should be tied back.

Hot Chicken Dip

Ingredients:

1 (10½ oz.) can cream of mushroom soup
1 (5 oz.) can chunk white chicken, or cooked, diced chicken
1 (8 oz.) pkg. cream cheese
1 (2 oz.) pkg. slivered or sliced almonds
1 (2 oz.) can sliced mushrooms
½ tsp. Worcestershire sauce
⅛ tsp. garlic powder
⅛ tsp. pepper

Directions:

1. Combine all ingredients in a 1-quart saucepan, fondue pot, or small crockpot.
2. Cook over medium heat until blended and heated thoroughly.
3. Serve hot with crackers or corn chips. Serves 4.

 If you have a fondue pot, use it to keep this dip warm. Keep cords and hot pots away from the reach of young children.

Spinach Mini Frittatas

Ingredients:

1 (10 oz.) pkg. frozen chopped spinach, thawed and drained
1½ c. part skim ricotta cheese
1 c. grated Parmesan cheese
4–6 (1 c.) fresh mushrooms, wiped and chopped
2 eggs
½ tsp. dried oregano
¼ tsp. salt

Directions:

1. Preheat oven to 375°.
2. Mix all ingredients in medium bowl.
3. Coat 36 miniature muffin cups lightly with cooking spray (or prepare in 3 batches of 12). Divide mixture among cups.
4. Bake 25 minutes. Remove from mold and serve with rubber spatula. Makes 36.

 Bake these in regular muffin pans for 12 lunch- or brunch-size servings. You can freeze them, then briefly reheat in microwave.

 Here is an easy, nearly fool-proof way to hard-boil eggs: Cover desired number of eggs with cold water in a non-aluminum saucepan. Heat to boiling. Turn off the heat and cover the pan, leaving the pan on the burner. Set timer for 40 minutes. When the timer goes off, drain the eggs and cover them immediately with cold water. Refrigerate.

 Do you know how to tell which eggs are fresh and which are hard-boiled? Spin the eggs on the counter. The hard-boiled egg will spin smoothly, while the fresh egg will wobble. Why do you think that happens? (In the hard-boiled egg the yolk has become solid and is the center of gravity. In the fresh egg the yolk remains fluid.)

Becky's Mexican Dip

Ingredients:

2 (8 oz.) pkgs. cream cheese
1 can Hormel hot chili, no bean
1 chopped onion
¼ c. chopped black olives
½ c. Monterey Jack cheese, grated
tortilla chips

Directions:

1. Preheat oven to 350°.
2. Mix cream cheese, chili, onion, and olives; pour into casserole dish. Top with cheese.
3. Bake until hot (about 20 minutes). Serve hot with tortilla chips. Serves 6–8.

 Label each dish you take to a potluck or to a friend. Put a piece of masking tape on the bottom, with your name written on it in permanent ink. When your friend flips it over to put it into the dishwasher, she'll see your name and remember to give it to you.

Crab Cake Muffins

Ingredients:

½ c. margarine (soft)
1 jar Old English cheese spread
1 (6 oz.) can crab meat, drained
1 T. mayonnaise
garlic salt to taste
6–8 English muffins (split in half)

Directions:

1. Preheat oven to 350°.
2. Mix all ingredients together and spread on English muffin halves.
3. Bake 20 minutes. Cut into quarters. Makes 48–64 quarters.

Take these muffins to a potluck for a change from the usual chips-and-salsa fare!

A spoonful of sugar is the best cure for hiccups. The trick is to swallow the sugar dry, without letting it melt in the mouth. Something about getting it down will usually eliminate the hiccups. (Even if it doesn't work, kids rarely mind this cure.)

Sausage Balls

Ingredients:

1 lb. bulk sausage, mild or hot
1 (10 oz.) pkg. extra sharp cheese, grated
1 tsp. paprika
3 c. Bisquick
cayenne pepper

Directions:

1. Preheat oven to 350°.
2. Have sausage and cheese at room temperature (but don't leave sausage out of refrigerator longer than a half hour). Combine and mix well.
3. Add paprika, cayenne pepper, and Bisquick; mix well.
4. Roll into small balls; place an inch apart on a baking sheet and bake 12–15 minutes, or until lightly browned. Do not overbake. After baking, may be frozen on baking sheet, then transferred to a freezer bag for use later.

 Whenever you're expecting out-of-town company or the holidays are approaching, prepare some of these appetizers to pull from the freezer at the spur of the moment.

 Thank you, God, for Everything
Thank you for the world so sweet,
Thank you for the food we eat.
Thank you for the birds that sing.
Thank you, God, for everything.
Amen.

        —Author unknown

Artichoke Cheese Dip

Ingredients:

½ c. sour cream
½ c. mayonnaise
1 c. grated Parmesan cheese
1 (8 oz.) pkg. cream cheese
1 clove garlic, minced
½ tsp. seasoning salt
1 (14 oz.) can artichoke hearts

Directions:

1. Preheat oven to 325°.
2. Mix all ingredients together; press into a baking dish.
3. Bake 30–35 minutes. Serve on crackers. Serves 6.

 This creamy, rich dip is addictive. You can adjust the flavors according to your tastes. For example: (1) add chopped green onions for additional flavor and color; (2) garnish with minced parsley; (3) add a dash of Tabasco if you like a hotter tang; or (4) substitute low-fat variations for sour cream, mayonnaise, and cream cheese.

 Artichokes are good sources of vitamins A and C, and calcium, iron, and potassium. They are moderately high in protein and carbohydrates, and low in fiber and fat.

Mexican Layer Dip

Ingredients:

2–3 large avocados, mashed
⅛ tsp. garlic powder
⅛ tsp. garlic salt
1 T. lemon juice
2 T. mayonnaise
1 can fat free refried beans
1 (8 oz.) container sour cream
1 (8 oz.) jar picante sauce
3 small chopped tomatoes
2½ c. shredded cheddar cheese

Directions:

1. Mix first 5 ingredients and set aside.
2. Spread beans in a small skillet (cast iron if you have one). Warm on medium heat until cooked through.
3. Spread avocado mixture over beans; layer sour cream, picante sauce, tomatoes, and cheese. Serve with chips. Serves 6–8.

 Think of a friend who is in the thick of an overwhelming project — wall papering a bedroom, mopping up water from the basement, cleaning out a grandmother's home. Double this recipe and take one to her for a needed break — "just because."

Cheese Blintze

Ingredients:

1 loaf sandwich bread (square slices)
1 (8 oz.) pkg. cream cheese, softened
¼ c. sugar
1 egg yolk
1½ sticks margarine or butter, melted and cooled
1¼ c. sugar
5 tsp. cinnamon
¾ c. powdered sugar

Directions:

1. Preheat oven to 400°.
2. Cut crusts off bread slices; roll thin with rolling pin.
3. Blend cream cheese with sugar and egg yolk; spread on each slice of bread.
4. Roll into shape of crepe. Dip each into melted margarine and roll in a mixture of cinnamon and sugar.
5. Place on cookie sheet. Bake 7–10 minutes or until brown. Sprinkle with powdered sugar. Serve warm.

 If you want to prepare these ahead for company, freeze them on a cookie sheet before baking. When frozen, remove from cookie sheet and store in zip-closure bag. When ready to serve, bake at 400° for 15–20 minutes. Serve with fresh fruit for a change of pace.

 Here is lots of rolling pin and dipping fun for children!

Cheese Ball

Ingredients:

1 (3 oz.) pkg. dried beef (found in prepackaged lunch meat
    section)
1 medium onion, cut fine
1 (8 oz.) pkg. cream cheese, softened
parsley, chopped fine

Directions:

1. Finely chop dried beef and onion (food processor works great).
   Combine with cream cheese.
2. Roll into ball and roll ball in parsley. Serve with crackers. Serves
   6.

 Let us acknowledge the LORD; let us press on to acknowledge him. As surely as the sun rises, he will appear; he will come to us like the winter rains, like the spring rains that water the earth (Hosea 6:3).

Vegetable Pizza

Ingredients:

2 pkg. Pillsbury crescent rolls
1 (8 oz.) cream cheese, softened
1 c. cottage cheese
¾ c. mayonnaise
1 pkg. Hidden Valley Ranch dry dressing
½–1 c. each (or to cover as desired) finely chopped broccoli, cauliflower, tomatoes, onions, bell peppers, carrots, and fresh mushrooms

Directions:

1. Place rolls flat on cookie sheet, pressing together all perforated edges. Bake according to directions and cool.
2. Mix together cheeses, mayonnaise, and dressing. Spread over cooled dough.
3. Sprinkle with chopped vegetables, putting tomatoes on last. Cut into squares. Makes 64 squares.

 Children can rinse the broccoli, cauliflower, tomatoes, carrots and bell peppers, and wipe the mushrooms with a moist paper towel. Even finicky eaters will be more interested in veggies if they help prepare them.

Chinese Fried Walnuts

Ingredients:

6 c. water
4 c. walnuts
½ c. sugar
vegetable oil
sprinkle of salt

Directions:

1. Prepare about 1½ hours before serving or up to 2 weeks ahead.
2. In 4-quart saucepan over high heat, bring water to boiling. Add walnuts and heat to boiling; cook 1 minute.
3. Rinse walnuts under running hot water; drain.
4. In large bowl gently stir warm walnuts with sugar, using a rubber spatula, until sugar is dissolved.
5. Meanwhile, heat about 1" salad oil in saucepan to 350° on deep fat thermometer.
6. With slotted spoon add about half the walnuts to oil. Fry 5 minutes or until golden, stirring often.
7. Remove walnuts from oil with slotted spoon; place in coarse sieve over bowl to drain.
8. Sprinkle very lightly with salt; toss lightly to keep nuts from sticking together.
9. Transfer to absorbent brown grocery bag to cool.
10. Fry remaining walnuts; drain, sprinkle with salt, toss, and cool.
11. Store in tightly covered container. Makes 4 cups.

 These nuts make a flavorful snack; try using pecans or other favorite nut.

 Use these nuts to dress up a simple green salad for guests. Mix salad greens, fresh apple chunks, raisins, cheese, and a mild vinegar/oil dressing. Sprinkle nuts on top for a delicious salad.

Easy Crab Meat Spread

Ingredients:

8 oz. cream cheese, softened
2 T. mayonnaise
2 T. Worcestershire sauce
2 tsp. lemon juice
¼ tsp. garlic salt or flakes
1 small onion, minced
½ (12 oz.) bottle chili sauce
1 (4½ oz.) can crab meat or ½ lb. imitation crab meat
1 T. chopped parsley

Directions:

1. Blend cream cheese, mayonnaise, Worcestershire sauce, lemon juice, garlic, and onion.
2. Spread in shallow serving dish and refrigerate about 1 hour.
3. After mixture sets, spread with chili sauce.
4. Top with crab meat and sprinkle with chopped parsley. Serve with crackers!

 Chili sauce can also be used to jazz up hamburgers, as a shrimp cocktail sauce, in chili, or to make homemade Thousand Island dressing.

Shrimp Croissant Sandwich

Ingredients:

1 ½ c. baby shrimp
¼ c. mayonnaise
2 T. dill pickle relish
¼ tsp. onion salt
4 leaves of lettuce
4 slices of tomato
4 croissants
2 T. butter

Directions:

1. Mix first 4 ingredients; refrigerate until ready to use.
2. Slice croissants. Spread with butter and broil lightly in oven or toaster oven. Spread mixture on croissant.
3. Top with a leaf of lettuce and slice of tomato. Serves 4–6.

 For an elegant touch use the mini-croissants available at many grocery stores.

 If you want to liven up a flat-tasting recipe, try one of these: salt and pepper, Tabasco sauce, soy sauce, vinegar, or lemon juice.

Apple Dip

Ingredients:

1 (8 oz.) pkg. cream cheese
¾ c. brown sugar
¼–½ c. chopped pecans (or crushed dry roasted peanuts)
1 tsp. vanilla
3 apples

Directions:

1. Blend together well. (The food processor does this in a flash!)
2. Serve with fresh, sliced apples. Serves 6.

 Non-fat cream cheese does not blend smoothly in this recipe.

 Sprinkle apple slices with lemon juice to prevent discoloring. Try pears or other fruit with this dip.

 Children love to dip. Kids who won't touch fruits or vegetables in a normal presentation will dive into apples with caramel dip or veggies with salad dressing.

Peanut Butter Pretzels

Ingredients:

1 (10 oz.) bag pretzel rods or logs
peanut butter
Rice Krispies
raisins
mini-chocolate chips or cookie sprinkles

Directions:

1. Spread the top two-thirds of a pretzel log with peanut butter.
2. Sprinkle Rice Krispies onto a cookie sheet.
3. Roll the coated log in the cereal.
4. Dot with raisins, mini-chocolate chips, or sprinkles.

 Rolling the pretzels in the cereal, and arranging the raisins or the chocolate chips on them, are great exercises in small motor development for your child. Encourage them to help and praise their efforts!

 Here are some lunch treats you might pack: cheese and crackers, dried fruit, raisins, popcorn, string cheese, frozen grapes, and vegetables with salad dressing dip.

Chocolate Covered Pretzels

Ingredients:

1 (14 oz.) large twist
1 (12 oz.) pkg. white chocolate chips
colored decorator sugar (opt.)

Directions:

Melt white chocolate morsels in microwave (melt ⅓ of the package at a time in a 2-cup Pyrex container). Dip pretzels halfway in and place on waxed paper; shake colored sugar on top. Let dry. Store in airtight containers.

This is a perfect recipe for kitchen helpers. When they dip the pretzels, talk about what "halfway" means. Demonstrate ¼, ½, ⅓ fractions. Doing and seeing is the best way for children to learn.

Remember this one when it's your turn to bring snacks for your child's class, or for Christmas giving.

Microwave Caramel Corn

Ingredients:

3–4 qts. popped popcorn
1 c. brown sugar
1 stick margarine
¼ c. light corn syrup
½ tsp. salt
½ tsp. baking soda

Directions:

1. Pop 3–4 quarts of your favorite popcorn.
2. In large bowl microwave brown sugar, margarine, corn syrup, and salt on high heat until melted, 2–3 minutes.
3. Boil mixture for 2 minutes. Remove from the microwave.
4. Stir in baking soda; stir until foamy.
5. Pour mixture over the popped corn.
6. Place coated popcorn in a brown grocery bag. Fold down top edge to close and microwave for 1½ minutes on high.
7. Remove from microwave and shake bag very well. Microwave for another 1½ minutes.
8. Shake again and cook 1¼ minutes more.
9. Pour into serving bowl, or quickly form into popcorn balls or cakes. Makes 12 popcorn balls.

 Cooked sugar mixtures get very hot. The bowl and bag may be quite hot to the touch. Be careful.

Gopher Food

Ingredients:

1 c. brown sugar	6 c. Cheerios
⅔ c. light corn syrup	1½ c. peanut butter
1 tsp. vanilla	1–2 c. flaked coconut (opt.)
1 c. semisweet chocolate chips	

   (or ½ c. chocolate chips and ½ c. peanut butter chips)

Directions:

1. Combine brown sugar and corn syrup in saucepan and heat on medium-high to boiling, stirring frequently. Remove from heat and transfer to a large mixing bowl.
2. Add vanilla and peanut butter and mix until smooth.
3. Stir in Cheerios and coconut. Add chocolate chips, stirring until chips are melted.
4. Let cool and eat. Serves 10.

 This unusual name means you'll really "go-for" this food!

 To keep brown sugar soft — or to soften hardened brown sugar — add a slice of apple or crust of bread to the sugar container. Keep brown sugar in a tightly sealed jar or zip-closure bag.

 An Early Saint's Prayer
Give Us, O Lord, thankful
hearts, which never forget
Your goodness to us.
Give us, O Lord, grateful
hearts, which do not waste
time complaining.
       —Saint Thomas Aquinas

Puppy Chow

Ingredients:

1 c. peanut butter
1 c. chocolate chips
¼ lb. butter
8 c. Chex cereal (any flavor)
2 c. powdered sugar

Directions:

1. Melt peanut butter, chocolate chips, and butter together 2 minutes in microwave on high.
2. Mix in cereal.
3. Place mixture in brown paper grocery bag. Add powdered sugar; shake well to coat. Serves 12.

 Take a bag of your child's favorite snack on the next long car or airplane trip. Fidgety children will appreciate the diversion.

Valleys of

VEGGIES, SALADS, AND SIDES

Delicious Chicken Salad

Ingredients:

2 c. steamed fresh broccoli, still crunchy
2 c. sweet seedless red grapes
2 c. cooked chicken, cubed
½ c. fresh celery, chopped
½ c. Miracle Whip or mayonnaise
fresh lettuce

Directions:

1. Combine all ingredients except lettuce in a bowl. (Can add more salad dressing to make creamier.)
2. Chill one hour and serve on crisp, fresh lettuce on individual plates. Serves 4.

 Ask your kitchen helper to remove the red grapes from their stems.

 Steaming is an excellent way to prepare vegetables, maintaining their color and crispness. Boil water in the bottom of a large sauce pan (enough to come up to the bottom of the steaming container), insert a perforated steaming container, cover the pan at once and cook 3 to 5 minutes longer than you would have cooked the same vegetables in boiling water. You can also use the microwave for steaming vegetables. Place them in a shallow dish, add a few tablespoons of water, and cover with plastic wrap. Cook, turning once, until vegetables reach desired doneness.

Ranch Taco Chicken Salad

Ingredients:

1 lb. boneless, skinless chicken breasts, cut into strips
1 T. chili powder
1 T. vegetable oil
1 (16 oz.) pkg. salad greens
½ c. salsa
½ c. Ranch dressing
1 c. shredded cheddar cheese
½ c. crushed tortilla chips

Directions:

1. Cook chicken with chili powder in oil in nonstick skillet for 8 minutes or until chicken is done.
2. Toss chicken, greens, salsa, dressing, and cheese in large bowl.
3. Top with chips before serving. Serves 6.

 Fiesta Crayons — You'll need: broken crayons (all colors), muffin tin, and foil. Line muffin cup with foil. Preheat oven to 300°. Have your child remove all paper from crayons. Fill each cup halfway with 1" long pieces of broken crayon. Place in oven and watch carefully — they melt quickly. Don't let them melt completely — just until blended. Don't stir. Remove from oven and let cool. When cool, remove from pan and peel off foil. Little hands can grab these chunks, or if you wish, break them into smaller pieces. Let your child see what pretty designs she can make with these unusual colors!

Tuna Pasta Salad with Herb Vinaigrette

Ingredients:

4 T. light olive oil or vegetable oil, divided
3 T. red wine vinegar
1 clove garlic, minced
1 tsp. dried basil
¼ tsp. oregano
1¼ c. small pasta shells (measured before cooking)
½ lb. frozen green beans
½ tsp. salt
1½ c. broccoli flowerets
1 red or green pepper, cut into strips
1 (6 oz.) can chunk white tuna

Directions:

1. Combine 3 tablespoons oil, vinegar, garlic, basil, and oregano in a small jar or plastic container with lid. Cover and shake well.
2. Cook pasta according to package directions. Drain pasta and place in large bowl. Add 1 T. oil; toss to coat.
3. Bring 2 quarts water to boil in large saucepan. Add beans and salt. Boil 2 minutes; drain.
4. Add beans, broccoli, red or green pepper, and tuna to pasta.
5. Shake dressing and pour over salad; toss to coat.
6. Season with additional basil and oregano to taste. Serve in bowl lined with greens if desired. Serves 6.

 Vinegars add a perky, clean taste to salads that brings out the flavor of foods without adding salt or fat. Experiment with types of vinegars, such as balsamic or tarragon. The classic proportions for dressing a salad is three parts salad oil to one part vinegar.

Seafood Pasta Salad

Ingredients:

½ c. mayonnaise
¼ c. zesty Italian dressing
¼ c. grated Parmesan cheese
2 c. corkscrew (rotini) noodles
1½ c. imitation lobster (or any 12 oz. seafood)
2 c. fresh broccoli
½ c. green pepper
½ c. chopped tomato
¼ c. sliced green onions

Directions:

1. Cook noodles according to package directions. Drain.
2. Parboil broccoli.
3. Combine first three ingredients. Put remaining ingredients in a salad bowl and toss with dressing. Serves 4–6.

 Think of three or four women would you really like to have over for lunch? Serve Seafood Pasta Salad on a bed of lettuce accompanied with melon and warm rolls. Oh, yes, don't forget a little something chocolate.

 Have you wondered what imitation lobster and crab are made of? It's Pollock, a white Alaskan fish, with flavorings added.

Toasted Pecan Bleu Cheese Salad

Salad:

equivalent of 1 (2 lb.) bag prepared mixed greens
5 oz. bleu cheese, crumbled
1 large tomato or ½ pt. cherry tomatoes
½ sweet red onion, sliced into thin rings

Toasted pecans:	*Vinaigrette:*
¼ cup butter, melted	1 T. Dijon mustard
4 tsp. Worcestershire sauce	4 T. red wine vinegar
1 T. garlic salt	2 tsp. sugar
½ tsp. hot sauce	1 tsp. salt
4 cups pecan halves	½ tsp. cracked black pepper
	1 T. parsley
	½–1 c. olive oil

Directions:

Preheat oven to 375°.

1. Mix together ingredients for vinaigrette. Set aside.
2. Mix together ingredients for toasted pecans. Bake 5–10 minutes, stirring and checking often.
3. Layer salad ingredients in bowl or 9" x 13" glass dish in order. Drizzle dressing over top. Serve immediately. Serves 6–8.

 You can freeze and store chicken or vegetable stock for use in soups or stews. Save cooked vegetables in the freezer until you have enough to prepare a stock for soup.

 Experiment with this beautiful fresh salad. Use different combinations of greens: romaine, spinach, butter lettuce, or read leaf lettuce. Or if convenience rules, use a 2-lb. bag of prepared mixed greens. A rough rule of thumb is that a handful of greens serves one person. Try the toasted pecans in other salads and dishes as well.

Chinese Cole Slaw

Ingredients:

1 large green cabbage shredded or 1 (16 oz.) pkg. preshredded cabbage
1 bunch green onions, chopped
2 pkgs. Ramen noodle soup, chicken flavor
2 oz. slivered almonds, toasted
½ c. sesame seeds, toasted

Dressing:

¾ c. vegetable oil
6 T. white vinegar
4 T. sugar
1 tsp. salt
1 tsp. pepper
both soup flavor packets from Ramen noodles

Directions:

1. Crush Ramen noodles. Set aside soup flavor packets for dressing.
2. Mix salad ingredients. Mix dressing ingredients and refrigerate; pour on before serving. Serves 8.

 Give everyone at the table a lump of clay or Play Doh. Ask them to shape something they saw today and tell about it. This is for everyone — Mom, Dad, even Gramps!

 A garlic press makes super "hair" with Play Doh. And the bits of colored Play Doh in your pressed garlic afterward will be a reminder of your child!

Pea Salad

Ingredients:

1 (20 oz.) bag frozen peas
1 celery stalk, chopped
8 hard-boiled eggs, sliced
1 bunch radishes, sliced
1 bunch green onions, sliced
½–1 c. mayonnaise (or to taste)
salt and pepper to taste

Directions:

Mix all ingredients together 1 hour before serving. (Peas are added frozen; they thaw quickly.) Serves 12.

 One mom put eggs on to boil, forgot about them, and went to bed. In the morning they were on the ceiling.

 One evening before bed, try this experiment with your child. Slice a stalk of celery halfway up the stalk. (Be sure you use a piece of celery that has the green leafy top in place.) Fill two glasses with colored water (red in one glass, blue in the other works well). Place each "leg" of the celery stalk in a glass of water. In the morning you will see how the celery has been able to "drink" the colored water up the stalk.

Spinach Salad with Poppy Seed Dressing

Ingredients:

1 cup pecan halves
3 T. butter, melted
1 bag spinach
2 c. strawberries, sliced

Dressing:

1 tsp. salt
⅓ c. white wine vinegar
½ c. sugar
1 c. light olive oil
1½ T. poppy seeds
1 tsp. dry mustard
1½ T. minced onion

Directions:

1. Combine all dressing ingredients in covered container. Shake well and refrigerate overnight.
2. Coat pecans with melted butter and bake at 350° for 10 minutes.
3. Wash spinach well and remove stems. At serving time toss spinach with poppy seed dressing, adding a little at a time until the salad is just coated and not too oily (you may have extra).
4. Top with strawberries and pecans. Serves 10.

Strawberries are America's favorite berry. Although they're available year-round in stores, strawberry season is April through July for most local strawberries, which are the best. Try to use strawberries within 24 hours. If you have some leftover, serve them for dessert with shortcake (see recipe on box of Bisquick) and cream. Top with Devonshire Cream recipe on page 27.

Catalina Spinach Salad

Ingredients:

2 (10 oz.) bags spinach, torn
2 large tomatoes, diced
2 (8 oz.) cans sliced water chestnuts, drained
2 c. bean sprouts
2 hard-boiled eggs, chopped
12 bacon strips, cooked and crumbled

Dressing:

½ c. vegetable oil
¼ c. ketchup
¼ c. red wine vinegar
¼ c. finely chopped onion
3 T. sugar
2 tsp. Worcestershire sauce
½ tsp. salt

Directions:

1. Combine dressing ingredients in a jar with tight lid; shake well.
2. Combine remaining ingredients in large salad bowl; add dressing and toss. Serve immediately. Serves 6–8.

 When you take a salad to a potluck or to give to a friend, transport the dressing ingredients in a small, tightly covered container and the salad ingredients in a large zip-closure bag. When you arrive, you can toss all ingredients in your or a friend's salad bowl.

Sue's Spinach Salad

Ingredients:

1 head of lettuce
1 bag of fresh spinach
1 medium red onion, diced
½ lb. bacon, fried and crumbled
3 hard-boiled eggs, sliced
1 c. mayonnaise
½ c. sugar
½ c. white vinegar

Directions:

1. In a large bowl tear pieces of lettuce and spinach.
2. Add onions, bacon, and eggs. Toss gently.
3. In a separate bowl, make a dressing of mayonnaise, sugar, and vinegar. Pour over salad mixture just before serving.

 Try a new recipe once a week. Use magazines, favorite cookbooks, and friends for inspiration.

Mandarin Orange Salad

Ingredients:

Almonds:

¼ c. sliced almonds
4 tsp. sugar

Salad:

¼ bunch Romaine lettuce, torn into bite-sized pieces
¼ head lettuce, torn into bite-sized pieces
2 medium stalks celery, chopped (1 c.)
2 green onions with tops, thinly sliced
1 (11oz.) can mandarin orange segments, drained

Sweet and sour dressing:

¾ cup vegetable oil
1½ T. sugar
4 T. white vinegar
½ tsp. salt
dash cayenne pepper
dash pepper
1 T. snipped parsley

Directions:

1. In a small saucepan heat the almonds and sugar together on medium low heat until the sugar melts and caramelizes on almonds.
2. Toss remaining salad ingredients except mandarin oranges and place in large zip-closure bag.
3. Make sweet and sour dressing and refrigerate.
4. Just before serving, add sweet and sour dressing and mandarin oranges to bag contents and shake until everything is thoroughly coated. Serve in salad bowl. Serves 6.

 Get into the habit of washing fresh greens as soon as you bring them home from the store (or in from the garden), so that you can make a salad anytime. Rinse them well in cold water, let them drip dry in a colander (or spin in a salad crisper), and store in the refrigerator until they're crisp. Store in batches of leaves wrapped in paper towels and sealed in zip-closure bags from which the air has been pressed out. Do not pack leaves tightly together.

 This is a delicious choice for guests. You can have the entire salad ready ahead of time, and mix just before serving.

Seven Layer Salad

Ingredients:

1 c. cauliflower, chopped
1 c. celery, chopped
1 c. green onions, chopped
1 (10 oz.) pkg. frozen peas, thawed
2 c. lettuce, chopped
1 c. tomatoes, chopped
chopped carrots (opt.)
chopped green pepper (opt.)
1 c. Miracle Whip or mayonnaise
8 oz. cheddar cheese, grated
7 strips bacon, fried and crumbled

Directions:

1. Place alternating layers of vegetables in a large bowl; spread Miracle Whip over top.
2. Sprinkle top with grated cheese and crumbled bacon.
3. Cover salad and refrigerate. Will keep in refrigerator for several days. Serves 8.

 This salad is a classic potluck dish. It also serves well for a holiday buffet, because it can be made in advance.

A. J.'s Green Bean and Feta Salad

Ingredients:

1½ lbs. fresh green beans
½ c. red onion, finely chopped
½ c. feta cheese, crumbled
½ c. walnuts, toasted and chopped

Vinaigrette:

1 T. lemon juice, freshly squeezed
1 T. white wine vinegar
1 tsp. Dijon mustard
¼ tsp. dried basil, crumbled
¼ tsp. sugar
¼ tsp. salt
¼ tsp. black pepper
⅓ c. olive oil

Directions:

1. Plunge beans into a large pot of rapidly boiling water. Cook 5 minutes or until just tender, yet slightly crisp.
2. Meanwhile, prepare a large bowl of ice water. Drain beans and plunge into ice water until cool. Drain and pat dry with paper towels.
3. Combine lemon juice, vinegar, mustard, basil, sugar, salt, and pepper in a small bowl. Slowly whisk in olive oil until thickened and thoroughly blended.
4. Place beans on a serving platter and drizzle vinaigrette over them.
5. Top with red onion, feta cheese, and walnuts. Serve immediately or cover and chill for several hours. Serves 8–10.

Immersing cooked vegetables in ice water immediately after cooking is known as "refreshing" them. This not only stops cooking instantly, it also sets the color. Use this "flash cooking" method on fresh vegetables served as appetizers. The vegetables will be bright in color, and won't dry out on the tray.

 Green or snap beans, formerly called string beans because their strings had to be removed, have been hybridized so that in most cases they now only have to have their ends snapped off. Tipping beans is a great job for a kitchen helper sitting at the table.

A Different Apple Salad

Ingredients:

1 Red Delicious apple, cored and chopped
1 Golden Delicious or Granny Smith apple, cored and chopped
½ c. seedless raisins
½ golden raisins
½ c. celery, chopped
½ c. cheddar cheese, cubed
¼ c. macadamia nuts, chopped (or pecans or walnuts)
juice of 1 orange
8 oz. vanilla yogurt
cinnamon (opt.)

Directions:

1. In medium bowl, combine apples, raisins, celery, cheese, and nuts.
2. Blend orange juice into yogurt. Pour over salad and toss well. Sprinkle with cinnamon, if desired. Serves 10–12.

 When you give a luncheon or dinner, do not invite friends, your brothers or relatives, or your rich neighbors; if you do, they may invite you back and so you will be repaid. But when you give a banquet, invite the poor, the crippled, the lame, the blind, and you will be blessed. Although they cannot repay you, you will be paid at the resurrection of the righteous (Luke 14:12–14).

Swiss Beans

Ingredients:

4 T. butter or margarine, divided
2 T. flour
1 tsp. salt
¼ tsp. pepper
1 tsp. sugar
1 T. grated onion
1 c. sour cream
2 (14½ oz.) cans French-style green beans
1 c. mozzarella or Swiss cheese, grated
1 c. cornflakes, crushed

Directions:

1. Preheat oven to 350°.
2. Melt 2 tablespoons butter in saucepan over medium heat. Stir in flour, salt, pepper, sugar, and onion.
3. Add sour cream to mixture and simmer for 1–2 minutes until thick. Fold in green beans.
4. In 1½-quart casserole dish, layer beans and cheese, ending with cheese on top.
5. Pour remaining melted butter on top and sprinkle with cornflakes. Cook 30 minutes uncovered. Serves 4–6.

 Remember, it warms a child from the inside out when you prepare a dish you know they like!

Delicious Broccoli Casserole

Ingredients:

1 large head fresh broccoli
1 (10½ oz.) can cream of mushroom soup
2 T. minced onion
¼ c. sharp cheddar cheese, shredded
½ c. sour cream
1½ T. Dijon mustard
1 T. horseradish
½ c. melted butter
1 c. Pepperidge Farm stuffing

Directions:

1. Preheat oven to 350°.
2. Cut off broccoli florets and smaller stems, discarding large stems. Parboil broccoli. Drain and place in 9" x 9" casserole dish.
3. Mix all ingredients except broccoli, melted butter, and stuffing on top of stove on medium heat until melted. Pour sauce over broccoli.
4. Lightly toss stuffing mix in melted butter. Sprinkle over top of sauce.
5. Bake covered for 30 minutes, until bubbly. Uncover for last 15 minutes. Serves 6.

 Parboiling means to add the vegetables to boiling water — a little at a time so as not to disturb the boiling — and cook until just under done. If you want to save the broccoli to use later, plunge it into cold water after parboiling. Store in a tightly sealed zip-closure bag.

Swiss Broccoli Casserole

Ingredients:

1 (16 oz.) bag frozen chopped broccoli
2 boiled eggs, sliced
1 (10½ oz.) can cream of celery soup
⅔ can of milk
1 (12 oz.) pkg. shredded Swiss cheese (or cheddar)
1 small can French-fried onions (found in canned vagetable
   section)

Directions:

1. Preheat oven to 325°.
2. Microwave or parboil broccoli (4 minutes in microwave or 6–7 minutes on top of stove.) Place in ovensafe casserole dish.
3. Cover with egg slices.
4. Combine soup and milk in separate bowl and pour over top. Add French-fried onions next and top with Swiss cheese.
5. Cover and bake 25 minutes. Serves 8.

 Newly married, my husband and I wanted to establish our own special holiday traditions. We decided to make duck for Christmas dinner. I eagerly set about finding special ways to cook Christmas Duck. I soon settled upon a recipe called "Flaming Duck" that sounded intriguing.

On Christmas Day, the exciting moment arrived for me to set the duck aflame. The instructions said to warm brandy and pour it over the duck, then set a lit match toward the top. I carefully poured ¼ cup of cheap brandy into my metal measuring cup and turned on the gas burner to warm it. I had just turned toward my husband and announced, "Get ready, this is just about warm enough," when — poof! — the brandy ignited at about the same time the handle of the metal cup got too hot to hold, causing me to throw the flaming brandy to the floor.

Within seconds, the carpet was ablaze with orange, red, and blue flame. I raced to the phone and called the fire department. In the short time it took them to arrive, however, the alcohol in the brandy had burned away and the flames went out, leaving no trace of fire. I was left with no proof to support my claim except for the bottle of brandy in my one hand and a ¼ cup measuring cup in the other.

The firemen were convinced of something, but I don't believe it was the danger to my kitchen.

Butternut Squash Bake

Ingredients:

⅓ c. butter or margarine, softened
¾ c. sugar
2 eggs
1 (5 oz.) can evaporated milk
1 tsp. vanilla
2 c. butternut squash, cooked and mashed

Topping:
½ c. Rice Krispies cereal
¼ c. brown sugar, packed
¼ c. chopped pecans
2 T. butter or margarine, melted

Directions:

1. Preheat oven to 350°.
2. In a mixing bowl cream butter and sugar. Beat in eggs, milk, and vanilla. Stir in squash (mixture will be thin).
3. Pour into a greased 7" x 11" baking pan. Bake uncovered for 45 minutes or until almost set.
4. Combine topping ingredients; sprinkle over casserole. Return to oven for 5–10 minutes or until bubbly. Serves 6–8.

 Butternut squash is a winter squash shaped like a large pear with buttery tan skin. Most winter squash is best baked. To eat on its own, cut the squash into halves or quarters and place in a baking dish, cut side down. Bake at 375°–400° until tender, at least 45 minutes. Remove the squash from the oven and scoop out the flesh.

 In the fall, let your children explore the interesting colors and shapes of squashes and gourds in your supermarket. Buy a few for an autumn centerpiece.

Tangier Island Corn Pudding

Ingredients:

1 (15 oz.) can creamed corn
1 (12 oz.) can evaporated milk
½ c. sugar
2 eggs
3 T. cornstarch
1 T. butter, melted

Directions:

1. Preheat oven to 350°.
2. Mix all ingredients together. Pour into lightly buttered 1-quart casserole dish.
3. Bake 1 hour or until set in center. Serves 4.

 Do you have a single-parent friend who is approaching a birthday? Invite her children over and let them help you prepare a special meal for Mom — complete with candles and cake.

 Suppose a brother or sister is without clothes and daily food. If one of you says to him, "Go, I wish you well; keep warm and well fed," but does nothing about his physical need, what good is it? (James 2:15–16).

Baked Corn Pudding

Ingredients:

1 (16 oz.) bag frozen corn
1 c. cracker crumbs, crushed
½ c. onion, chopped fine
½ c. American cheese, cubed
1 tsp. salt
2 eggs, beaten
2 T. butter, melted
1 c. milk

Directions:

1. Preheat oven to 350°.
2. Combine ingredients. Pour into greased 1½-quart casserole.
3. Bake 50–55 minutes. Serves 6.

 Make pizza with your kids. Make pizza dough in a bread machine or buy premade pizza dough. Divide the dough so each child gets a portion and her own pan to put it on. Then let them spread on sauce, sprinkle on mozzarella cheese, and add any other toppings you have on hand. Bake at 400° for 15 minutes and enjoy your creations.

Pineapple Casserole

Ingredients:

3 (15 oz.) cans chunky pineapple, drained
½ c. sugar
2 T. flour
1 c. sharp cheddar cheese, grated
1 sleeve Ritz crackers, crushed
¾ stick (6 T.) butter, melted

Directions:

1. Preheat oven to 350°.
2. Put drained pineapple chunks in greased 8" square or 1½-quart round baking dish.
3. Mix sugar and flour together and sprinkle over pineapple. Spread cheese over sugar and flour as next layer; then crushed crackers. Pour butter over top of crackers.
4. Bake 25 minutes. Serves 8–10.

 To crush crackers, seal them in a plastic bag and run a rolling pin over the bag.

 This is a delicious side dish for a ham or pork chop dinner.

Zucchini and Tomato Casserole

Ingredients:

4 small zucchini
4 small tomatoes
1 small onion
salt and pepper to taste
2 T. brown sugar divided
2 tsp. Italian seasoning, divided
¾ c. bread crumbs
¼ c. butter
1 c. grated cheddar cheese

Directions:

1. Preheat oven to 350°.
2. Thinly slice zucchini, tomatoes, and onion. Divide onion into rings.
3. Spray a deep casserole dish with nonstick spray. Layer half of the zucchini, half of the tomatoes, and half of the onion rings. Sprinkle with half of the salt and pepper, brown sugar, and seasoning. Then sprinkle layer of half each bread crumbs, butter, and cheese. Repeat layers.
4. Bake covered for 30 minutes. Uncover and continue baking for 45 minutes or until center is bubbling hot. Serves 8.

 To make bread crumbs, toast the heels of bread loaves, then tear them in pieces and pulse them in a blender or food processor.

 Make paper cup telephones! Punch a hole in the bottom of two paper cups. Tie a string through the hole and knot it on the inside of the cup. Play "phone" with your child.

Sweet Potato Casserole

Ingredients:

> 6 medium sweet potatoes or 1 (29 oz.) can sweet potatoes, drained
> ½ c. white sugar
> 2 eggs
> 1 tsp. vanilla
> ⅓ c. milk
> ½ c. margarine or butter, melted

> *Topping:*
> ⅓ c. brown sugar, packed
> ⅓ c. chopped pecans
> 2 T. flour
> 2 T. margarine or butter, melted

Directions:

1. Preheat oven to 350°.
2. Boil potatoes 45 minutes or until tender. Let cool; peel and mash.
3. Mix potatoes with all ingredients except topping and beat at medium speed until smooth.
4. Combine topping ingredients.
5. Spread the potato mixture in a lightly greased 9" x 13" pan; sprinkle topping over it. Bake 30 minutes. Serves 8.

 Alternate topping:
¾ c. crushed cornflakes
½ c. chopped walnuts
½ c. brown sugar
¾ stick butter

 A generous man will himself be blessed, for he shares his food with the poor (Proverbs 22:9).

Holiday Mashed Potatoes

Ingredients:

3 lbs. (about 12) medium potatoes, peeled and cooked
1 (8 oz.) pkg. cream cheese
¼ c. margarine or butter
½ c. sour cream
½ c. milk
2 eggs, beaten
¼ c. onion, chopped fine
1 tsp. salt
dash pepper
¼ tsp. ground nutmeg
pinch seasoned salt

Directions:

1. Using electric mixer, mash hot potatoes. Add cream cheese in small pieces. Add butter; beat well until cream cheese and butter are completely mixed. Mix in sour cream.
2. In a separate bowl mix milk, eggs, and onion together. Add to potatoes; beat until fluffy. Place in a greased pan. Sprinkle with seasoned salt.
3. Refrigerate several hours. Bake at 350° for 45 minutes. Serves 8–12.

 The beauty of this dish is that you can serve mashed potatoes without all the potato-peeling mess as your company arrives. This is a great holiday accompaniment to beef, pork, or poultry.

 Don't even think of stuffing all the potato peelings down the disposal at once, or celery (ever), or corn silk (unless you have a plumber in the family).

 Do you know why ham is a traditional Easter dinner choice? In days of old, hogs were slaughtered in the fall and hams were prepared for "curing." Cured hams were ready in the spring, just in time for Easter dinner.

Favorite Potluck Potatoes

Ingredients:

¼ c. butter, melted
½ c. chopped onion, chopped
1 c. sour cream
1 (2 lbs.) bag frozen, shredded hash browns, thawed
1 (10½ oz.) can cream of chicken soup
1 (10½ oz.) can cream of celery soup
8 oz. shredded cheddar cheese
2 c. crushed cornflakes, (opt.)

Directions:

1. Preheat oven to 350°.
2. Mix all ingredients and place in 9" x 13" pan.
3. Top with 2 cups crushed cornflakes, if desired. Bake 45–60 minutes. Serves 12–14.

 This is a potluck or "for company" classic. If you have any left over, press it into round patties and warm in a skillet or on a griddle the next morning for delightful potato pancakes. Top with applesauce.

Oven Taters

Ingredients:

2–3 lbs. white or red potatoes
1 tsp. Lawry's seasoned salt (or to taste)
½ tsp. pepper
¼ c. butter or margarine
4 oz. American cheese slices

Directions:

1. Preheat oven to 350°.
2. Clean skins of potatoes thoroughly; slice as for fried potatoes into baking dish. Sprinkle alternately with seasoned salt and pepper. Dot liberally with chunks of butter or margarine and add a little water.
3. Cover with foil. Bake 45 minutes.
4. Remove and add slices of cheese; return to oven for a few minutes, until cheese melts, 5–10 minutes. Serves 6.

Have a kitchen helper scrub those potatoes at the sink.

If you use a wooden cutting board, remember that because wood is porous, it can absorb odors, colors, flavors, and bacteria. It's best to use two wooden cutting boards: one for meat and poultry and the other for salads, fruits, and vegetables. Wash both after use with soapy water, rinse and wipe dry with a towel. The board you use for meat should occasionally be scoured with a paste made of baking soda and water, rinsing and drying as usual. Store wooden cutting boards vertically.

Sea of
SOUPS AND STEWS

Magic Beef Stew

Ingredients:

1 lb. stew beef	2 tsp. salt
3 stalks celery	½ tsp. pepper
1 onion	1 T. sugar
3 carrots	2 T. minute tapioca
3 potatoes	1½ c. tomato juice

Directions:

1. Preheat oven to 275°.
2. Cover bottom of heavy pan with meat. Cut and arrange vegetables on top. Combine dry ingredients and sprinkle on top of vegetables. Add tomato juice. Cover pan tightly with foil or lid. Bake 4 hours. Do not peek or stir. Serves 6.

 Stews are an excellent choice to serve to company because they may be made ahead, portions can be easily stretched, and the aroma is inviting.

 Long, slow cooking times will produce very tender meat. For stews, cut the vegetables into wedges, slices, or cubes of uniform size to assure even cooking.

 Tapioca, which acts as the thickening in this recipe, will keep on the pantry shelf for some time. Try the recipe on the box to make tapioca pudding for dessert—a kid favorite!

Taco Stew

Ingredients:

1 – 1 ½ lbs. lean ground beef
½ c. chopped onion
1 or 2 T. taco seasoning
2 (15 oz.) cans stewed tomatoes
1 (15 oz.) can red kidney beans, drained
2 c. shredded cheddar cheese
tortilla chips
½ c. sour cream
sliced black olives

Directions:

1. Brown ground beef with onion; drain.
2. Add taco seasoning, stewed tomatoes, and kidney beans. Bring to a boil. Reduce heat and simmer 30 minutes (or longer).
3. Spoon into bowls. Top with shredded cheese, sour cream, and black olives. Garnish with chips. Serves 4.

 A fun variation of Taco Stew is the "Taco Joe" or "Mexican Pile-On." Serve the stew and condiments in separate bowls and let each person build their own taco. Additional condiments include shredded lettuce, fresh chopped tomatoes, and salsa. Let your guests help by having them each bring a condiment.

 Most meat stews can be stored in the freezer for up to six months.

 Roll leftover in flour tortillas and microwave for a quick meal.

Cranberry Beef Stew

Ingredients:

2 lbs. boneless beef,
   cut in 1" cubes
2 T. vegetable oil
3 c. water
1 tsp. Worcestershire sauce
1 clove garlic, minced
1 bay leaf
2 tsp. salt
½ tsp. paprika
⅛ tsp. pepper

6 carrots, sliced (or use
   "baby" carrots)
1 lb. whole small onions, peeled
1 (16 oz.) can whole cranberry
   sauce
¼ c. cold water
2 T. cornstarch
½ tsp. Kitchen Bouquet (opt.,
   but adds color and intensifies
   flavors)

Directions:

1. Thoroughly brown meat on all sides in hot oil.
2. Add 3 c. water, Worcestershire sauce, garlic, bay leaf, salt, paprika, and pepper.
3. Cover; simmer for 1¼ hours, stirring occasionally.
4. Remove bay leaf. Add carrots, onions, and cranberry sauce.
5. Cover and cook 30–45 minutes or until meat and vegetables are tender.
6. Combine ¼ cup water, cornstarch, and Kitchen Bouquet. Stir into stew. Continue cooking, stirring until stew is thick and bubbling. Serves 8–10.

 Often, your supermarket butcher will cut meat into cubes for you at no extra charge.

 This sweet and tangy stew is a pleasant change of taste. Serve in bread bowls for a special touch.

Karol's Quick Chili

Ingredients:

1 lb. extra lean ground beef, browned
1 onion, chopped (or ¼ c. dried, chopped onion)
2 cloves garlic, minced (or 1 tsp. garlic powder)
½ tsp. cumin
2 dashes Tabasco sauce
2 (15 oz.) cans tomatoes with liquid
1 (6 oz.) can tomato paste
1 tsp. sugar
3 (15 oz.) cans small red beans, drained and rinsed
2 c. water
2 c. frozen corn
salt and pepper to taste

Directions:

1. In a large electric skillet add onion and garlic to the beef. Sauté until slightly translucent.
2. Add remaining ingredients in order and simmer, covered, for 25–45 minutes. Serve with tortilla chips or corn bread. Serves 6.

 This tummy-warming, one-dish meal is great after a day of outdoor winter fun. It's easy to vary the "heat" to suit family tastes by leaving out the Tabasco sauce or adding a 4-oz. can of green chilies.

 Add a little sugar to recipes with canned tomatoes to cut the acidic flavor.

 All thy children shall be taught of the LORD; and great shall be the peace of thy children (Isaiah 54:13 KJV).

White Chili

Ingredients:

4 (1 lb.) cans Great Northern beans, drained
3 (14½ oz.) cans chicken broth
1 c. water
1¼ c. onion, chopped
2 cloves garlic, minced
½ tsp. salt
2 c. chicken or turkey, chopped and cooked
1 (4 oz.) can chopped green chilies
1½ tsp. cumin
1 tsp. dried oregano
¼ tsp. Cayenne pepper
¼ tsp. ground cloves
¾–1 c. shredded Monterey Jack cheese

Directions:

1. Place all ingredients except cheese into large (5-quart) heavy pot.
2. Bring to a boil, reduce heat, and simmer at least 30 minutes.
3. Spoon into serving bowls. Top with cheese. Serves 6.

 Here is a hearty soup to make with leftover turkey after the holidays. You can use leftover gravy in place of some of the chicken broth.

 Being married only a few years, I was still a bit shy about my cooking ability. But I was confident about my mom's famous "paper bag" turkey. The object was to coat the inside of a paper bag with mayonnaise and cook your turkey inside the bag.

We were stationed on one of the naval bases in Puerto Rico. My husband invited a few single military men and women over for Thanksgiving dinner. Wanting to please, I began my dinner with gusto! A few hours later I smelled something burning and discovered my turkey, complete with paper bag baked on! I had forgotten the coating of mayonnaise!

Thinking quickly, I simply peeled the bag off the bird and served it with a smile. Everyone loved my "Hickory Smoked" turkey and thanked me over and over for my trouble.

Baked Potato Soup

Ingredients:

4–5 large baking potatoes
⅔ c. margarine or butter
⅔ c. flour
1½ qt. (6 c.) regular or low-fat milk
salt and pepper to taste
pepper
6 green onions, sliced thin
1 c. regular or nonfat sour cream
½ lb. crisp bacon, crumbled
6 oz. cheddar cheese, shredded

Directions:

1. Bake potatoes and remove pulp.
2. Melt margarine in large pot. Add flour; stir.
3. Gradually add milk; stir constantly until thickened (about 5 minutes).
4. Stir in all other ingredients. Thin with milk if reheated. Serves 10–12.

 When you serve baked potatoes, bake 4–5 extra so you can serve this soup the next night.

 For the beauty of the earth,
For the glory of the skies,
For the love which from our birth,
Over and around us lies,
Lord of all, to Thee we raise
This our hymn of grateful praise.

Words by Folliott S. Pierpoint
Music by Conrad Kocher

Potato Cheese Soup

Ingredients:

2 c. potatoes, peeled and cubed
½ c. carrots, chopped
½ c. celery, chopped
½ c. onion, chopped
3 c. water
2 tsp. chicken bouillon granules
¼ c. butter
¼ c. flour
1 tsp. salt
1 pint half and half
⅛ tsp. pepper
½ c. Swiss cheese, shredded
2 c. shredded sharp cheddar cheese (or more)

Directions:

1. Cook vegetables in water and bouillon until tender.
2. Melt butter in separate pan. Add flour and salt and blend well.
3. Stir half and half in butter and flour mixture to thicken. Add to vegetables.
4. Stir pepper and cheeses in until cheeses melt. Do not let come to a boil. Serves 4.

 Cut the greens off carrots before storing them in the refrigerator. The greens drain carrots of moisture, making them thick and dry.

 Grow an indoor carrot plant with the thick top of a carrot. Pour ½" inch of water into a shallow dish. Place the carrot top in the water with the trimmed green end pointing up. Watch the greens resprout within a week.

Golden Cheese Soup

Ingredients:

¼ c. water
2 T. butter
1 (10 oz.) pkg. frozen corn
½ c. carrots, grated
¼ c. onion, chopped
⅛ tsp. pepper
2 (10½ oz.) cans cream of potato soup
2 c. milk
1 c. (4 oz.) grated cheddar cheese
½ c. (2 oz.) grated provolone cheese
1 c. broccoli florets (opt.)

Directions:

1. Bring water, butter, corn, carrots, onion, and pepper to a boil in a 3-quart saucepan. Cover and simmer 5 minutes.
2. Add broccoli and simmer 5 minutes more.
3. Stir in soup, milk, cheddar and provolone cheeses.
4. Heat, stirring occasionally until cheese melts and serving temperature is reached. Do not boil. Garnish with additional broccoli florets, if desired. Serves 4.

Soups or stews are a soothing meal to take to a family that has an illness or new baby. Pack along a loaf of French bread or corn bread, and some cookies or bars for dessert.

What is it that's so comforting about soup? At the dinner table, with company or just your family, discuss *your* comfort foods. What memories do you associate with them?

Cheeseburger Soup

Ingredients:

½ lb. ground beef
¾ c. onion, chopped
¾ c. shredded carrots, shredded
¾ c. celery, diced
1 tsp. dried basil
4 c. potatoes, peeled and diced
  (or a 32 oz. pkg. of frozen
  hash browns)
8 oz. processed American cheese, cubed (2 c.)
1½ c. milk
¾ tsp. salt
¼–½ tsp. pepper

1 tsp. dried parsley flakes
4 T. butter or margarine,
  divided
¼ c. all-purpose flour
3 c. chicken broth

Directions:

1. Brown beef in a 3-quart saucepan; drain and set aside.
2. In the same saucepan, sauté onions, carrots, celery, basil, and parsley in 1 tablespoon butter until vegetables are tender, about 10 minutes.
3. Add broth, potatoes, and beef; bring to a boil. Reduce heat, cover, and simmer for 10–12 minutes or until potatoes are tender.
4. Meanwhile, in a small skillet, melt remaining butter. Add flour, cooking and stirring for 3–5 minutes or until bubbly. Add to soup; bring to a boil. Cook and stir for 2 minutes.
5. Reduce heat to low. Add cheese, milk, salt, and pepper. Cook and stir until cheese melts. Serves 8–9.

 Try serving this soup in "bowls" of bread. This recipe freezes well, so double it and put half in the freezer for another night, or to take to another family.

Vegetable Cheese Soup

Ingredients:

1 qt. water
3 chicken bouillon cubes
1 c. carrots, chopped
1 c. celery, chopped
1 c. onion, chopped
1½ c. potatoes, diced
1 (16 oz.) pkg. California blend frozen vegetables (broccoli, cauliflower, carrots)
2 (10½ oz.) cans cream of chicken soup (or mushroom, broccoli, etc.)
1 lb. Velveeta cheese, cubed
salt and pepper to taste

Directions:

1. Dissolve bouillon in water; add carrots, celery, onion, and potatoes.
2. Cook in boiling water for 15 minutes.
3. Add California blend vegetables; cook 5–6 minutes.
4. Add cream soup; heat.
5. Add cheese; heat until melted. Serves 10.

 For pureed soup (great if children have trouble eating large pieces of vegetables), after all the vegetables have been added put mixture in food processor for a few rapid pulses, then proceed with the recipe. Pureed soup can be served in mugs with carrot or celery stalk stirrers.

Quick Soup

Ingredients:

1½ lbs. lean ground beef
½ c. onion, chopped
1 (11½ oz.) can V−8 vegetable juice
1 tsp. sugar
1 tsp. celery salt
½ tsp. seasoned salt
1 tsp. ground pepper
2 large potatoes, peeled and cubed
3 large carrots, sliced
2−3 parsnips, peeled and sliced

Directions:

1. Brown meat with onion until no pink remains in meat.
2. Add juice to meat; simmer; season to taste with seasonings.
3. About 30−45 minutes prior to serving, add vegetables. Cook until tender, but not mushy. Serves 6.

 Adapt this soup to your family and what's in your refrigerator. Add peas, turnips, celery, whatever you like. Don't shy away from trying parsnips. They're like white carrots and add a sweet flavor to the soup.

 Try substituting barley for the potatoes.

Beef and Cabbage Soup

Ingredients:

1 lb. ground beef
½ tsp. garlic powder
¼ tsp. pepper
3 carrots, sliced
1 (15 oz.) can kidney beans, drained
¼ head cabbage, chopped
1 (28 oz.) can whole tomatoes
1 whole tomato can of water
4 beef bouillon cubes
¼ c. orzo, or other small pasta

Directions:

1. In large soup pot, brown beef; drain off grease.
2. Add remaining ingredients except orzo. Bring to a boil; reduce heat and simmer for one hour.
3. During last 10 minutes add orzo. Serves 8.

 Let a child summon the family together with a dinner bell.

 If the soup is too salty, don't dump it until you've tried one of these cures: Add water to dilute salty flavor; add thin slices of potato to absorb the salt; or add fresh or canned tomatoes with a pinch of sugar.

The Best Minestrone Soup

Ingredients:

3 slices bacon, finely chopped
1 c. onion, chopped
1 c. celery, chopped
2 large cloves garlic, minced
1 tsp. basil leaves, crushed
1 (15 oz.) can beef broth
1 (10½ oz.) can bean with
 bacon soup
1 (10½ oz.) can tomato soup
1½ soup cans of water
1 (15 oz.) can Italian seasoned stewed tomatoes

1 tsp. sugar
½ c. uncooked small tube
 macaroni
½ tsp. salt
pepper to taste
1 c. cabbage, cut in long
shreds
1 c. zucchini, cubed

Directions:

1. In large pan brown bacon and cook onion and celery until translucent. Add garlic and basil; cook briefly until mixed well.
2. Add beef broth, soups, water, tomatoes, sugar, macaroni, salt, and pepper.
3. Bring to boil, cover and reduce heat; simmer 15 minutes.
4. Add cabbage and zucchini. Cook 10 minutes more, until vegetables are tender. Stir occasionally.
5. Serve with garnish of Parmesan cheese. Serves 8.

 This soup can be easily prepared in a crockpot. After step one add all ingredients to crockpot. Cover and cook on high 4–5 hours. Later in the day, prepare a green salad and some garlic bread.

 To remove unpleasant cooking smells or splatters from a microwave, place a cup with three parts water to one part lemon juice or vinegar inside. Cook for 8–10 minutes on lowest power. Wipe up microwave afterward.

Pumpkin Tomato Soup

Ingredients:

2 T. butter or olive oil
1 onion, chopped
1 (28 oz.) can pumpkin puree (preferably Libby's)
1 (15 oz.) can stewed tomatoes
4–6 cups chicken stock
2 T. maple syrup
salt and pepper to taste

Directions:

1. In a heavy soup pot, heat butter or olive oil. Add onion and sauté until soft and translucent.
2. Add chicken stock; bring to a boil and simmer 15 minutes.
3. Remove onions. In blender, combine onion, pumpkin, and tomato; puree.
4. Add pumpkin mixture to chicken stock and heat through. Add maple syrup, salt, and pepper. Serve with Parmesan cheese or sour cream. Serves 8–10.

 For a festive holiday look, serve Pumpkin Tomato Soup in a hollowed-out pumpkin with parmesan cheese grated on top.

 For a unique pasta sauce, omit the chicken broth and don't puree the onion, pumpkin, and tomato.

 To roast pumpkin seeds, remove seeds from pumpkin. Wash the seeds and drain them in a colander. Soak seeds in salt water for several hours or overnight. Drain. Sprinkle with additional salt if desired. Bake in shallow baking pan at 325° about 1 hour, turning seeds every 15 minutes until golden brown.

Split Pea Soup

Ingredients:

1 lb. dried split green peas, rinsed
8 c. water
1½ c. onion, chopped
2 garlic cloves, pressed
1 c. celery, chopped
1 c. carrots, peeled and chopped
1 large potato, peeled
   and chopped
2 bay leaves

¼ tsp. marjoram
¼ tsp. thyme
¼ tsp. basil, chopped
3–4 T. parsley, chopped
pinch red pepper
dash black pepper
diced ham to taste (opt.)
salt to taste (opt.)
1 c. croutons (approx.)

Directions:

Place all ingredients except croutons in a large crockpot. Turn on high for 8 hours, or overnight. Serve with croutons sprinkled on top. Serves 6–8.

Discuss over dinner the expression "fog thick as pea soup." Have your children ever experienced it? Talk about weather: your favorite weather, the scariest storm you've been through, what you like best to eat in what types of weather.

To prepare Split Pea Soup without a crockpot, soak the peas in water at least 8 hours; drain. (Place soaked peas in a blender or food processor and chopped for finer consistency.) Add all ingredients and cook over stove top in large pot, stirring frequently for two hours. Serve Split Pea Soup with corn bread instead of croutons. Dip or crumble the bread in the soup.

Three Bean Soup

Ingredients:

¼ c. bulgur
1 ¼ c. carrots, chopped
1 ¼ c. celery, chopped
1 medium to large onion
1 large clove garlic, chopped
1 (28 oz.) can tomatoes
1 (15 oz.) can kidney beans
1 (15 oz.) can black-eyed peas
1 (15 oz.) can northern beans
1 (11 oz.) can whole kernel corn
1 ½ tsp. Spice Island Italian herb seasoning (or mix a pinch
   each oregano, marjoram, thyme, summer savory, basil, rosemary, and sage)
1 ½ T. sugar
1 tsp. salt (or to taste)
1 bay leaf
water (as much as desired)

Directions:

1. Soak bulgur in ½ cup water for 30 minutes.
2. Sauté carrots, celery, onion, and garlic clove 5–8 minutes.
3. Add rest of ingredients except bulgur and cook 30 minutes.
4. Add the soaked bulgur and cook another 30 minutes or longer.
   Stir often to prevent sticking. Serves 12.

 Bulgur is a cracked-wheat grain.

 Serve leftover Three Bean Soup over baked potatoes.

R.D.'s Boardwalk Clam Chowder

Ingredients:

1 T. vegetable oil
1 onion, chopped
1 stalk celery, diced
2 T. parsley, minced
1 potato, with skin, cubed
1 carrot, sliced
1 (24 oz.) can chicken broth (low-salt)
2 c. nonfat evaporated milk, divided
2 T. flour
1 T. cornstarch

¼ tsp. salt
½ tsp. black pepper
2 (6½ oz.) can clams
   (undrained)
2 T. dry sherry (opt.)

Directions:

1. Sauté onions, celery, and parsley in oil until onions are translucent.
2. Add potatoes and carrots; cook a few minutes.
3. Add chicken broth and simmer 15 minutes. Mix in 1½ cup evaporated milk and heat through. Add clam juice.
4. Combine flour, cornstarch, salt, and pepper with remaining ½ cup milk. Bring soup to a boil and add flour mixture. Cook until thickened and flour taste is gone.
5. Add clams and sherry; stir well. Serves 6.

 Do you know the difference between Manhattan Clam Chowder and New England Clam Chowder? Manhattan usually includes a tomato base and New England does not. Think red for Manhattan, white for New England.

 You may substitute chicken bouillon for broth and salt.

Corn Crab Chowder

Ingredients:

¾ c. onion, chopped
3 c. potatoes, peeled and diced
1½ c. water
1½ tsp. salt
¼ tsp. ground pepper
¼ tsp. dill weed
2 T. bacon bits
1 (16 oz.) can creamed corn
10 oz. imitation crab
4 c. milk
1 (10½ oz.) can cream of celery soup

3 T. butter, divided
1½ T. flour
1 T. chopped parsley
dash paprika

Directions:

1. In large pot place onion, potatoes, water, salt, pepper, dill, and bacon bits. Cover and simmer 15 minutes, until potatoes are tender.
2. Add corn, crab, milk, and soup; heat gently.
3. Blend 1½ tablespoons butter and flour; add to soup. Stir and cook until thick.
4. Dot with remaining butter, and sprinkle with chopped parsley and paprika when serving. Serves 8–10.

Sit your child on the counter so you can look directly into his eyes. Tell him how happy you are that he is your child. (This works well for husbands too).

You can substitute ham or bacon for the crab. Serve with grated cheddar on top.

Veggie Ham Chowder

Ingredients:

1 c. carrots, diced

1 small onion, chopped

1 (16 oz.) can green beans, drained (or use frozen)

1 (16 oz.) can creamed corn

1 c. milk

1 c. celery, chopped

1 c. chopped ham

1 (10½ oz.) can cream of mushroom soup

3 (14½ oz.) cans chicken broth

3 soup cans water

1 c. shredded cheddar cheese

¾ c. noodles or rice

1 pkg. au gratin potatoes

Directions:

1. Mix together all ingredients except potatoes. Bring to a boil; simmer for 2 hours until carrots are tender.
2. Add potatoes and sauce packet; simmer 1 hour more. Serves 10.

 Chowders need to ripen; they are usually better the second day.

 Don't be overwhelmed by a black, charred, burned-on pan. After soaking it in hot sudsy water, drain the pan. Sprinkle baking soda (cream of tartar if it's an aluminum pan) on the burned spots, add a little water, and bring the solution to a boil on the stove. Remove from heat, let the pan cool, and scrub as usual.

Italian Tortellini Soup

Ingredients:

1 lb. sweet Italian sausage   1 (16 oz.) can chopped tomatoes
1 c. onion, chopped   1 (8 oz.) can tomato sauce
2 cloves garlic, crushed   2 T. dried basil
5 c. beef stock   2 T. dried oregano
1 large carrot, peeled and sliced
1 (10–12 oz.) bag frozen or refrigerated cheese-filled
   tortellini (8 oz. if dried)
1 large zucchini, peeled and sliced

Directions:

1. Brown sausage with onion and garlic. Drain.
2. Add beef stock, tomatoes, tomato sauce, and spices; bring to low boil.
3. Add carrots; simmer 10–15 minutes.
4. Add tortellini and zucchini; continue cooking until tortellini is tender, 15–20 minutes. Ladle into soup bowls and top with a sprinkle of Parmesan cheese. Serves 8–10.

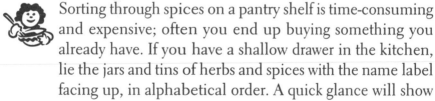

Sorting through spices on a pantry shelf is time-consuming and expensive; often you end up buying something you already have. If you have a shallow drawer in the kitchen, lie the jars and tins of herbs and spices with the name label facing up, in alphabetical order. A quick glance will show you whether you have a particular one or not.

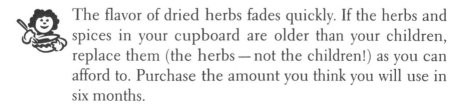

The flavor of dried herbs fades quickly. If the herbs and spices in your cupboard are older than your children, replace them (the herbs — not the children!) as you can afford to. Purchase the amount you think you will use in six months.

Chicken Tortellini Soup

Ingredients:

1 boneless, skinless chicken breast
2 c. water
1 small onion, chopped
2 stalks celery, chopped
2 c. frozen chopped spinach
2 (14½ oz.) cans chicken broth
¼ tsp. salt
¼ tsp. pepper
1 (8 oz.) pkg. frozen cheese tortellini

Directions:

1. Place chicken breast in large pot or crockpot and cover with 2 cups water; simmer until tender, approximately 1 hour. Shred cooked chicken breast with fork or large spoon.
2. Add remaining ingredients to crockpot, except tortellini; simmer an additional hour.
3. Cook tortellini according to package directions.
4. Add tortellini to soup prior to serving. Sprinkle each serving with grated Parmesan cheese. Serves 6.

 It's so easy to burn a hand or arm while cooking, particularly if you're in a rush. For a minor kitchen burn, do not remove shreds of tissue or break blisters. Immerse the burn in cold water (not ice water) until the pain subsides or apply a cold, clean washcloth that has been wrung out in ice water. Gently blot dry with sterile gauze or a clean cloth. Cover the burn loosely with a dry, clean dressing. Elevate burned arms or hands higher than the heart.

Chicken Gumbo

Ingredients:

1 onion, chopped
½ green pepper, chopped
1 clove garlic, minced
1 – 1½ c. water
1 (16 oz.) can diced tomatoes
1 (14 oz.) can cut okra, drained
1 (6 oz.) can tomato sauce
1 beef bouillon cube
rice, instant or regular for 4 servings

4 tsp. Worcestershire sauce
⅛ tsp. ground cloves
½ tsp. chili powder
1 bay leaf
salt and pepper to taste
3 c. water
2 c. chicken, cooked and
    diced

Directions:

1. Simmer onion, green pepper, and garlic in ½–1 cup water.
2. Add remaining ingredients except for rice. Bring to a boil; cover and simmer for 50 minutes, stirring occasionally.
3. Make rice according to package directions. Serve gumbo over rice in bowls. Serves 4.

 Kitchen shears cut chicken much more easily than a knife. Wash and dry shears carefully after use — especially after cutting raw chicken.

 I can do everything through him who gives me strength (Philippians 4:13).

Elegant Chicken Soup

Ingredients:

1 (14½ oz.) can chicken broth

4 c. water

1 (10½ oz.) can cream of chicken soup

2 c. chicken, cooked and cubed

1 c. chopped onion, chopped

1 c. carrots. sliced

½ c. cooking sherry

½ tsp. oregano

½ tsp. basil

2 cloves minced garlic

1 (13 oz.) pkg. frozen cheese tortellini

1 (10 oz.) pkg. frozen chopped broccoli, thawed

Directions:

1. Mix everything but broccoli and tortellini in large soup pot.
2. Bring to a boil; add tortellini and simmer 30 minutes.
3. Add broccoli and cook 10 more minutes. Serves 8.

 "Draw a Meal" is a great way to entertain your child while you fix dinner. Cover the table with a large sheet of paper, anchoring the corners with masking tape. Provide your child with crayons. Have him draw a place mat at the place where each family member sits, followed by a plate, napkin, flatware, and cup for each person.

As you prepare the meal, explain what you are making so your child can draw each dish and "serve" it to each person's plate. Ask her to serve appropriate portions for each member of the family.

Don't be surprised if you find blue tomatoes or red string beans!

 If you keep on hand a package of frozen tortellini, a jar of spaghetti sauce, and a loaf of French bread, you're moments away from a no-fuss meal!

Cream of Turkey Soup

Ingredients:

1 c. celery, finely diced
¼ c. onion, minced
3 T. butter
¼ c. flour
2 c. turkey broth
2 c. milk
1 c. grated fresh carrots
1 c. turkey, cooked and finely chopped
2 T. parsley, chopped
salt and pepper to taste

Directions:

1. Sauté celery and onions in butter about 5 minutes, until soft but not brown. Remove from heat.
2. Add flour and blend thoroughly. Add broth and milk to mixture all at once; stir until thick and smooth.
3. Add carrots and turkey meat. Cook about 10 minutes. Season with salt and pepper. Garnish with chopped parsley. Serves 6.

 My in-laws had been defrosting the turkey in the refrigerator. When they pulled the giblets from the cavity, they were still frozen. When they rinsed out the cavity, out jumped a frog, which they took to the pond in their backyard!

They called the supermarket where they'd purchased the turkey, who referred them to the packaging plant. The explanation they were given was that in the plant turkeys are processed on one conveyor belt and frog legs on the next. Somehow a frog went astray and survived being frozen. Yes, they did eat the turkey.

Tortilla Soup

Ingredients:

1 small onion, chopped
2 garlic cloves, mashed
1 (4 oz.) can green chilies, diced
4 T. vegetable oil, divided
1 (8 oz.) can stewed tomatoes
2 c. chicken broth
1 c. beef bouillon

1½ c. chicken, cooked and shredded (opt.)
1 tsp. cumin
1 tsp. chili powder
salt to taste
¼ tsp. pepper
2 tsp. Worcestershire sauce
4 corn tortillas
1 c. Monterey Jack cheese, shredded

Directions:

1. Using medium saucepan, sauté onion, garlic, and green chilies in 2 tablespoons oil until soft.
2. Add tomatoes, chicken broth, beef bouillon, and chicken; mix in seasonings and simmer for 1 hour.
3. Cut tortillas into quarters, then into ½" strips. Fry strips in 2 tablespoons hot oil until crisp; drain.
4. Add fried tortilla chips to soup and simmer 10 minutes. Ladle into bowls and top with shredded cheese. Serves 4.

 Let your child help clean up the kitchen. She can wipe counters with a big sponge and sweep the floor. A child-sized broom can do a surprisingly good job!

 Be sure pot handles on the stove are turned to the side or back, away from a child's reach.

Broccoli Ham Soup

Ingredients:

5 T. butter
4 T. flour
3 c. light cream or milk
2 ham steaks, trimmed and cut into bite-sized pieces
4 oz. Velveeta cheese
5 c. broccoli
5 c. chicken broth
salt and pepper to taste

Directions:

1. Melt butter in saucepan; blend in flour. Stir until smooth.
2. Whisk in milk slowly.
3. Add ham and simmer. Add cheese and heat until melted.
4. In soup kettle, cook broccoli in broth until tender. (If you want a finer soup, puree broccoli in blender with broth.) Add milk mixture to broccoli mixture. Add salt and pepper and simmer 30 minutes. Can also be made in crockpot. Serves 12.

 My son, who is seven, requests this soup on his birthday or if I'm going to be gone. My other children love it, too. I serve it with fruit and muffins.

 If you are going out to dinner and your child will be at home with a baby-sitter, try to sit at the table and talk about the evening with your child before you go.

Sam's Broccoli Cheese Soup

Ingredients:

2 (10 oz.) pkgs. frozen broccoli
2 T. flour
1 lb. Velvetta cheese
1 c. butter
1 c. milk
2 c. water
2 c. sour cream
dash pepper
1 (8 oz.) pkg. fine egg noodles (opt.)

Directions:

1. Cook broccoli until tender; mash with fork.
2. Cook noodles according to package directions; rinse and drain.
3. Blend remaining ingredients; add with noodles to broccoli.
4. Cook until cheese is melted and hot. Stir often. Serves 6.

 This rich, creamy soup is a favorite at brunches. Serve with fresh fruit.

 Experience family dining from another's perspective! Rotate seating positions at the table once in a while so each child will have a turn at the head.

Mountain

of

Main Dishes

Chicken á la King

Ingredients:

½ c. diced green pepper and/or red pepper
⅓ c. chopped onion
¼ c. butter or margarine
1 (10½ oz.) can cream of chicken soup
¾ c. milk
2 c. chicken, cooked and cubed
¾ c. shredded cheddar cheese
salt and pepper to taste

Directions:

1. In 10" skillet sauté green pepper and onion in butter. Stir in soup and milk; blend well. Stir in chicken and cheese.
2. Cook 5 minutes more or until heated through. Serve over biscuits, baked potatoes, shredded zucchini, or spaghetti squash. Serves 4.

 Create your own family traditions for meals — such as soup, salad, and muffins every Saturday night.

Chicken and Rice Casserole

Ingredients:

1 c. uncooked rice
1 (10½ oz.) can cream of mushroom soup
1 (10½ oz.) can cream of celery soup
1½ c. milk
2–3 lbs. chicken pieces
1 envelope dry onion soup mix

Directions:

1. Preheat oven to 350°.
2. Butter a 9" x 13" casserole dish. Mix rice, soups, and milk; pour into dish.
3. Place chicken pieces on top. Sprinkle with onion soup mix; cover with foil.
4. Bake 1½ hours. Serves 5.

 A pleasing plate includes at least three colors. This plate will need some help! Serve with green beans and cranberry sauce, or other colorful accompaniments.

Emilie's Favorite Chicken and Rice

Ingredients:

2 c. chicken, cooked and cubed
1 c. celery, chopped
1 c. rice, cooked
¾ c. mayonnaise
1 c. mushrooms, sliced
1 T. onions, chopped
1 tsp. lemon juice
1 tsp. salt (or to taste)
2 (10½ oz.) cans cream of chicken soup
1 (8 oz.) can sliced water chestnuts

Topping:
¼ c. butter, melted
½ c. sliced almonds
1 c. cornflakes, crushed

Directions:

1. Preheat oven to 350°.
2. Mix all ingredients except topping. Place in 2-quart casserole dish.
3. Mix topping ingredients and sprinkle over top.
4. Bake 35 minutes or until bubbly. Serves 6.

 You can use leftover cooked chicken, or if you have no time, buy a roasted chicken at the grocery store. Add green peas for a splash of color.

 Put the cornflakes in a zip-closure bag. Let your child help crush them with a rolling pin or using only their hands.

Baked Chicken and Stuffing

Ingredients:

- 4 boneless, skinless chicken breasts
- 4 slices Swiss cheese
- 1 (10½ oz.) can cream of chicken soup
- 2 c. Pepperidge Farm stuffing mix or 1 (6 oz.) pkg. Stove Top Stuffing
- ¼ c. butter or margarine
- ½ c. hot water

Directions:

1. Preheat oven to 325°.
2. Grease an 11" x 7" baking pan.
3. Layer chicken breasts, then Swiss cheese, then soup.
4. Melt butter; stir in water and stuffing. Sprinkle stuffing over soup.
5. Bake covered for 45 minutes.
6. Uncover and bake 15 minutes longer to brown the top. Serves 4.

 Create a few familiar, standard menus. Don't feel guilty about preparing the same two or three dishes together. You're actually creating memories of "comfort foods" for your children. We all have favorite memories of menus or foods that bring a sense of consistency and continuity to our busy lives.

 You can also prepare this dish in the microwave: cover with wax paper and cook on high 10–15 minutes, until done.

Crunchy Chicken Rolls

Ingredients:

3 oz. cream cheese, softened
2 c. chicken, cooked and chopped
1 T. chopped chives
2 T. milk
½ tsp. salt
2 pkg. (8) crescent rolls
¼ c. margarine or butter, melted
½ c. herb seasoned stuffing crumbs

Directions:

1. Preheat oven to 350°.
2. Mix cream cheese, chicken, chives, milk, and salt in a medium bowl (mixing with your hands works best).
3. Unroll crescent rolls. Each tube will contain 4 rectangles of dough with a diagonal perforation. Press dough along perforations so dough won't separate into triangles.
4. Place about ¼ cup chicken mixture onto center of each rectangle of dough. Fold dough over filling and pinch edges to seal tightly.
5. Dip each roll in margarine and roll in stuffing crumbs. Place on baking sheet and bake 20 minutes. Serves 4–6.

 Serve these rolls on a parents' night out. Open a can of cranberry sauce for a colorful accompaniment.

 "We're having leftovers" rarely sounds like music to a family's ears. The trick to using leftovers is to use them in a completely new dish. Roast chicken or turkey comes back as Tetrazzini or Chicken Rolls; ham encores in Split Pea Soup.

Chicken Croissant

Ingredients:

1 (8 oz.) pkg. cream cheese, softened
2 (10½ oz.) cans cream of celery soup
8 skinless, boneless chicken breast halves
8 croissants, split in half

Directions:

1. Preheat oven to 375°.
2. Mix cream cheese with soup. Lay chicken breasts in 9" x 13" baking dish. Cover with soup mixture.
3. Bake 45 minutes to 1 hour. When done, serve on croissants. Serves 8.

 To lighten up this dish, make it with Neufchâtel cheese and serve on English muffins or toast.

 She opens her arms to the poor and extends her hands to the needy (Proverbs 31:20).

Chicken Pot Pie

Ingredients:

1 (10½ oz.) can cream of potato soup
1 can Veg-All, drained, or frozen mixed vegetables, thawed
2 c. chicken, cooked and diced
½ c. milk
½ tsp. salt
¼ tsp. thyme
¼ tsp. pepper
2 (9") pie crusts, unbaked

Directions:

1. Preheat oven to 375°. Spread crust in 9" pie pan.
2. Combine all ingredients except crusts. Pour into unbaked pie crust.
3. Cover with top crust. Crimp edges to seal. Slit top crust to vent.
4. Bake 40–45 minutes. Cool 10 minutes before serving. Serves 4–6.

 One time I put my wooden recipe box on a stove burner, then turned that burner on instead of the burner I meant to use. My two-year-old son ran into the living room, looked at me with big round eyes, and shouted, "Fire, Mommy!"

Easy Chicken Tomato Pie

Ingredients:

3 c. chicken, cooked and diced
1 c. onion, chopped
1 c. celery, thinly sliced
3 medium tomatoes, chopped and drained
1½ c. shredded Swiss cheese
2¼ c. milk
¼ c. butter, melted
5 eggs
1¼ c. Bisquick
½ tsp. garlic salt

Directions:

1. Preheat oven to 350°.
2. Grease 9" x 13" baking dish.
3. Layer chicken, onion, celery, tomatoes, and cheese in dish.
4. Beat remaining ingredients in blender or with wire whip until smooth; pour into dish.
5. Bake 40–45 minutes or until knife inserted in center comes out clean. Cool 5 minutes. Serves 12.

 Kids enjoy trying to crack eggs. If you have some extra — and extra patience — let your child crack the eggs for this dish. Remember to wash hands after handling poultry or eggs.

Creamy Chicken Enchiladas

Ingredients:

8 chicken breasts, cooked and cubed
2 (10½ oz.) cans cream of chicken soup
1 (4 oz.) can green chilies
1 pt. sour cream
1 c. shredded cheddar cheese
5 green onions, chopped
10–12 flour tortillas

Directions:

1. Preheat oven to 350°.
2. Mix chicken with cream of chicken soup. Add green chilies, sour cream, ½ cup cheddar cheese, and green onions.
3. Fill flour tortillas with 2 tablespoons each of filling and roll up. Place seam side down in 9" x 13" pan.
4. Spread leftover mixture on top of tortillas and sprinkle with remaining cheddar cheese.
5. Bake 20–25 minutes. Serves 6–8.

 Even though green chilies are very mild, some children may not like them. To "de-spice" this dish, either eliminate the green chilies or add them to the mixture that goes on top. That way a child with a sensitive palate can scrape them off his or her portion.

Chicken Sour Cream Enchiladas

Ingredients:

16 oz. sour cream, divided
2 c. chicken, cooked and chopped
8 oz. shredded cheddar cheese, divided
2 c. salsa, divided
2 T. chopped cilantro
1 tsp. ground cumin
10 (6") flour tortillas
1 c. lettuce, chopped (opt.)
1 c. tomato, diced (opt.)

Directions:

1. Preheat oven to 350°.
2. Mix 1 cup sour cream, chicken, 1 cup cheese, ½ cup salsa, cilantro, and cumin.
3. Spoon approximately ¼ cup mixture onto each tortilla. Roll up and place in greased 9" x 13" baking dish.
4. Top tortillas with remaining salsa. Cover.
5. Bake 30 minutes. Sprinkle with remaining cheese. Return to oven until cheese melts.
6. Serve with remaining sour cream, lettuce, and tomato. Serves 6.

 Talk about breads from different countries with your child (pita bread from the Middle East, French bread from Europe, pumpernickel bread from Germany). If you have time, check a reference book for facts about Mexico and how tortillas are made.

South of the Border Chicken

Ingredients:

3 lb. boneless chicken
1 pkg. corn tortillas
1 onion, chopped
1 bell pepper, chopped
1 T. chili powder
1 lb. cheddar cheese
1 (10½ oz.) can cream of mushroom soup
1 (10½ oz.) can cream of chicken soup
1 (10 oz.) can El Paso tomatoes with green chilies

Directions:

1. Preheat oven to 350°.
2. Bake boneless chicken, covered, until no longer pink inside — about 40 minutes. Save broth. Cool chicken and dice.
3. Dip uncooked tortillas in chicken broth.
4. Combine chicken, onion, bell pepper, and chili powder.
5. In a greased 9" x 13" casserole dish layer 4 tortillas, chicken mixture, and cheese, repeating layers 3 times.
6. Combine soups and tomatoes with green chilies. Pour mixture over top. Bake 45 minutes. Serves 6–8.

 Make a jigsaw puzzle sandwich with your child using one piece of dark bread, one piece of white bread, and your choice of filling. Press a cookie cutter into the center of the sandwich. Remove the cut-out piece, flip it over, and insert it back into the sandwich, so that the center design is the opposite color of the bread surrounding it.

Chicken, Cheese, and Pasta

Ingredients:

1 – 1 ½ lbs. boneless chicken breast, cubed
¼ c. water
2 medium onions, chopped
garlic to taste
1 (14 oz.) can spaghetti sauce
1 (16 oz.) can stewed tomatoes
8 oz. pkg. pasta shells
¼ lb. provolone cheese, sliced
¼ lb. mozzarella cheese, sliced
1 pt. sour cream

Directions:

1. Preheat oven to 350°.
2. Cook chicken in about ¼ cup water in skillet treated with non-stick spray. Add onions, garlic, spaghetti sauce, and tomatoes. Simmer 20 minutes.
3. Cook pasta shells until tender; place half the shells in casserole dish.
4. Cover shells with half the tomato mixture. Spread with sour cream and cheeses. Repeat.
5. Bake covered for 30 minutes. Remove cover and bake until slightly brown. Serves 6–8.

 If you use a wooden cutting board for cutting meat, in addition to washing it in soapy water and drying it with a towel you should occasionally scour it with a paste made from water and baking soda. Rinse and dry as usual.

Crockpot Chicken Fettuccine

Ingredients:

2 whole boneless, skinless chicken breasts, halved
2 T. olive oil
¼ c. green onions, chopped
1 medium garlic clove, minced
1 (14.5 oz.) can chopped tomatoes
1 T. basil
1 tsp. salt
½ c. heavy cream
2 egg yolks
½ c. grated Parmesan cheese
8 oz. fettuccine
1½ c. fresh mushrooms, sliced

Directions:

1. In skillet, brown chicken in olive oil.
2. Place chicken in crockpot. Add green onions, garlic, tomatoes, basil, and salt. Cover and cook on low 5 hours or until chicken is done.
3. Remove chicken and cut into pieces. Return chicken pieces to pot. Stir in cream, egg yolks, and Parmesan cheese. Cover and cook on high 30 minutes to thicken.
4. While sauce is thickening, cook fettuccine according to package directions; drain.
5. Add fettuccine and mushrooms to sauce. Cover and cook on high 30–60 minutes. Serves 6.

 When you transport a dish in a large pot, set the covered pot in a heavy cardboard box not much bigger than the pot. Place the box on the floor of the car. The crockpot and its contents will ride more securely.

Chicken Spaghetti

Ingredients:

6 boneless, skinless chicken breast halves, cooked and cubed (save broth)
2 bell peppers, chopped
1 large onion, chopped
1 clove garlic, minced
3 T. salad oil
1 (26 oz.) can tomatoes
1 (10½ oz.) can tomato soup
1 lb. spaghetti

1 (8 oz.) can mushroom stems and pieces, drained
1 lb. sharp cheddar cheese, grated
salt and pepper to taste
1 T. Worcestershire sauce
1 (2.25 oz.) jar sliced black olives
⅓ c. Parmesan cheese (approx.)

Directions:

1. Preheat oven to 350°.
2. Bake chicken, covered, until no longer pink inside — about 40 minutes; save broth.
3. Cool chicken and dice.
4. Sauté peppers, onion, and garlic in oil. Add tomatoes and soup; simmer until thick.
5. Meanwhile, cook spaghetti in reserved chicken broth and water according to package directions; drain. Set aside in large bowl.
6. Add mushrooms, cheese, salt, pepper, Worcestershire sauce, and diced chicken to the cooked spaghetti.
7. Add olives to sauce and serve over spaghetti. Sprinkle with Parmesan cheese. Serves 8.

 To serve Chicken Spaghetti for company, prepare the sauce the day before or in the morning, but don't add the olives or Parmesan cheese until you heat it to serve.

If you cook the spaghetti but then need to "hold" it until serving time, drain the spaghetti and rinse under tepid water. Toss with 1 T. vegetable or olive oil to keep it from sticking together.

Stuffed Chicken Shells

Ingredients:

2 whole chicken breasts
2 boxes stuffing mix (chicken flavor)
1 T. Miracle Whip
1 box jumbo pasta shells or lasagna noodles
2 (10½ oz.) cans cream of chicken soup
1 soup can water

Directions:

1. Preheat oven to 350°.
2. Cook chicken and cut into little pieces.
3. Cook stuffing according to package directions.
4. Cook pasta shells or lasagna according to package directions until a little under done.
5. Mix together chicken, stuffing, and Miracle Whip. Stuff shells with mixture, or if using lasagna noodles, spread mixture on layers of noodles as you would for lasagna.
6. Mix soup with one can of water. Pour over shells or lasagna.
7. Bake in two 9" x 9" casserole dishes for 30 minutes and serve. Serves 10.

 Prepare this large, family-pleaser in two square casserole dishes. Take your child with you to deliver one to an elderly friend or relative, and let your child's presence further brighten their day!

 When you visit elderly relatives or neighbors, ask them to tell you what life was like when they were your age. Some things have changed a lot — and some things that children like to do may not be all that different. (Mom, make a real effort to introduce your child to people of all ages. Your children's lives will be enriched).

White Lasagna

Ingredients:

4 boneless, skinless chicken breast halves, cooked

2 c. ham, cooked and chopped

9 lasagna noodles

6⅓ T. butter or margarine, divided

1 (8 oz.) pkg. fresh mushrooms, sliced

⅓ c. butter or margarine

⅓ c. all-purpose flour

3 c. milk

1½ c. Parmesan cheese, freshly grated

½ c. whipping cream

¾ tsp. dried basil

½ tsp. salt

¼ tsp. pepper

Directions:

1. Preheat oven to 350°.
2. Cut cooked chicken into bite-sized pieces and place in a large bowl; add in chopped ham and mix.
3. Cook noodles according to package directions; drain.
4. Melt 1 tablespoon butter or margarine in a large skillet over medium-high heat; add mushrooms and sauté until tender. Drain. Stir mushrooms into meat mixture; set aside.
5. Melt 5⅓ T. butter in skillet; add flour and cook 1 minute, stirring constantly. Gradually stir in milk; cook, stirring constantly about 3 minutes or until bubbly.
6. Stir in Parmesan cheese, whipping cream, basil, salt, and pepper. Cook until cheese has melted and mixture is thickened.
7. Add meat mixture to cheese sauce. Stir well.
8. Spread one third of meat mixture into a greased 9" x 13" baking dish; top with 3 noodles. Repeat layers twice.
9. Bake covered for 30 minutes. Remove from oven and let stand 10 minutes before serving. Serves 12.

 When hosting dinner party for adults, six is a congenial number of guests at the table. This is enough for lively interaction, but not so many that not everyone can participate in the conversation.

Kerry's Chinese Chicken

Ingredients:

½ c. vegetable oil
1 tsp. chicken bouillon granules
1–2 T. soy sauce
½ tsp. garlic powder
1 lb. boneless chicken, cut into chunks
1 lb. fresh mushrooms
1 green pepper, sliced
½ head of cabbage, shredded
1 onion, chopped
1 medium carrot, peeled and shredded
6 servings rice or Chinese noodles

Directions:

1. Heat oil in wok on medium high. Mix in bouillon, soy sauce, and garlic powder. Add chicken and cook until tender (about 10 minutes).
2. Remove chicken with slotted spoon. Set aside.
3. Add remaining ingredients to wok; cook 5 minutes.
4. Add chicken back in; cook and stir 5 more minutes. Serves 6.
5. Serve over rice or Chinese noodles.

 Have the children think up "blessings." Write their blessings on strips of paper and place one under each cookie served for dessert.

 To add color and nutrition to this or other stir-fry dishes, add Chinese pea pods and cherry tomatoes.

Cantonese Chicken Breasts

Ingredients:

6 chicken breasts
½ c. apricot preserves
⅔ c. crushed pineapple, undrained
⅔ c. brown sugar, packed
3 T. lemon juice
1⅓ T. prepared mustard
1 T. soy sauce

Directions:

1. Preheat oven to 375°.
2. Bake chicken breasts 45 minutes, covered; drain off broth.
3. Mix rest of ingredients together; pour over chicken breasts.
4. Bake an additional 30 minutes or until tender. Serves 6.

 Avoid seasoning meat with salt before cooking. It draws out the moisture and will leave you with "parched" poultry. Try pepper, basil, tarragon, or oregano according to your tastes. Lemon pepper might work well in this recipe.

Serve this dish with rice and snow peas for a colorful, easy dinner.

Honey Barbecue Chicken and Ribs

Ingredients:

1 c. ketchup	1 tsp. dry mustard
½ c. water	1 tsp. salt
¼ c. vinegar	¼ tsp. pepper
1 tsp. garlic salt	3 lbs. "pick of the chick"
½ c. honey	chicken pieces
1 T. Worcestershire sauce	2 lbs. pork spare ribs

Directions:

1. Preheat oven to 375°.
2. Mix all ingredients except meat.
3. Place meat in large roasting pan. Pour sauce over meat.
4. Bake covered for 60 minutes; turn meat over and bake uncovered 45 minutes. Serves 8.

 Try pork "baby back ribs" or meaty "country-style" ribs. The combination of chicken and ribs in this recipe provides something for everyone.

Marinated Grilled Chicken

Ingredients:

1½ c. vegetable oil
¾ c. soy sauce
¼ c. Worcestershire sauce
2 T. dry mustard
1 T. pepper
⅓ c. lemon juice
2½ tsp. salt
½ c. wine vinegar
1½ T. parsley
1–2 garlic cloves, minced
3–4 lbs. chicken pieces

Directions:

1. Mix ingredients. Pour over chicken pieces in zip-closure bag or nonmetal bowl.
2. Marinate chicken in refrigerator at least 1 hour.
3. Grill or broil. Serves 5–6.

 If you use this marinade for grilled chicken, marinate the chicken in the refrigerator in a covered nonmetal dish or zip-closure bag. Pour off and reserve marinade and bake the chicken, covered, at 325° for 40 minutes. Then grill the chicken until done, basting with marinade for the final few minutes. Discard remaining marinade.

Easy Italian Microwave Chicken

Ingredients:

½ c. Italian flavored bread crumbs
2 T. Parmesan cheese
6 boneless chicken breast halves
¼ c. mayonnaise

Directions:

1. Combine bread crumbs and Parmesan cheese.
2. Cover chicken breasts with mayonnaise; roll in crumbs.
3. Arrange in microwave dish and cook 9–10 minutes on high or until no longer pink. Serves 6.

 This recipe is so simple you can easily use a little helper. Try working at the table instead of at the counter so your child can sit and work.

 Learn about Italy. Look it up on the map, read a book about all the art from Italy. Make an Italian flag out of colored paper for a centerpiece at dinner. At dinner, talk about what you've learned.

Hunter Chicken

Ingredients:

8 chicken thighs, skinned, or 4 boneless, skinless chicken
breasts
¼ c. flour
1 tsp. basil leaves
¼ tsp. garlic powder
¼ tsp. pepper
1 T. vegetable oil
1 (10½ oz.) can golden mushroom soup
1 (14½ oz.) can stewed tomatoes
1 small carrot, sliced
1 medium zucchini, sliced

Directions:

1. Coat chicken with flour, basil, garlic powder, and pepper. Cook in oil on medium high 10 minutes or until brown, turning chicken once. Remove and set aside.
2. Combine soup, tomatoes, and carrot. Heat to boiling in skillet.
3. Return chicken to skillet; cover; cook on low for 15 minutes.
4. Stir in zucchini; cover; cook 10 minutes or until chicken is done. Serves 4–6.

 When cooking potatoes, start raw potatoes in cold water so all the potatoes cook evenly. If you add them to already boiling water, the outside of the potatoes will become soft and the inside will still be crunchy.

 Let them give thanks to the LORD for his unfailing love and his wonderful deeds to men, for he satisfies the thirsty, and fills the hungry with good things (Psalm 107:8–9).

Apricot Chicken

Ingredients:

1 (8 oz.) jar apricot preserves
8 oz. Catalina or French salad dressing
1 pkg. dry Lipton onion soup mix
1½ lbs. of boneless chicken breast

Directions:

1. Preheat oven to 350°.
2. Mix preserves, dressing, and soup mix; pour over chicken in 8" square baking dish and cover with foil.
3. Bake 1 hour or until chicken is tender. Serve the apricot sauce poured over rice. Serves 4.

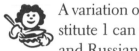 A variation of this popular recipe is cranberry chicken. Substitute 1 can whole cranberry sauce for the apricot preserves and Russian dressing for the Catalina or French dressing.

Chicken–Broccoli Casserole

Ingredients:

4 boneless chicken breasts
1 box frozen broccoli spears
2 T. lemon juice
1 (10½ oz.) can cream of
    chicken soup

½–1 tsp. curry (or to taste)
½ c. mayonnaise
½ c. Swiss cheese, grated
4 servings rice

Directions:

1. Preheat oven to 350°.
2. Bake chicken, covered, until no longer pink inside — approximately 40 minutes; save broth. Cool chicken and dice.
3. Cook broccoli in reserved chicken broth.
4. Mix lemon juice, soup, curry, and mayonnaise (may add a small amount of milk to make more sauce).
5. Lay chicken and broccoli in casserole dish; pour sauce over it.
6. Top with grated cheese; bake 30 minutes. Serve over rice. Serves 4.

"What if . . . ?" Rehearsing potentially scary situations can help relieve parental anxiety and can equip a child to react with wisdom in an emergency. During a quiet moment, ask your child if she'd like to play the "what if" game. Begin with simple scenarios, like "What if the door was closed and you couldn't get into the house? What would you go?" Depending on the age of the child, go over the choices you want the child to consider (ring the doorbell, sit on the steps, go to the neighbors, etc.) Other questions might be: What if you were in the store, and you couldn't find Mommy, what would you do? What if the mean little girl at school hit you, what would you do?

Giving children knowledge strengthens their confidence, and this game gives you an opportunity to teach them what you want them to do.

Chicken L'Orange

Ingredients:

1 egg
⅓ c. orange juice
1½ c. herb seasoned stuffing mix, crushed
1½ tsp. paprika
1 T. orange peel, grated
1 tsp. salt
8 boneless, skinless chicken breast halves
6 T. margarine or butter, melted
orange slices, (opt.)

Directions:

1. Preheat oven to 375°.
2. Beat egg; add orange juice.
3. In another bowl combine stuffing, paprika, orange peel, and salt.
4. Dip chicken into egg mix, roll in crumbs; coat well.
5. Pour margarine into 9" x 13" pan. Place chicken in pan; turn once to cover both sides.
6. Bake uncovered for 45 minutes or until chicken is tender. Garnish with orange slices, if desired. Serves 6–8.

 When grating orange peel, use only the outside "orange" part of the peel. Avoid the white "pith," which is bitter.

 If you use chicken with the bones, be sure to increase baking time.

Microwave Onion and Cheese Chicken Bake

Ingredients:

6 chicken breasts, skinned and boned
4 T. butter
1 tsp. seasoned salt
1 tsp. seasoned pepper
½ lb. fresh mushrooms, quartered
1 (3 oz.) can French-fried onions
½ c. shredded Monterey Jack cheese
½ c. Colby cheese
½ c. shredded cheddar cheese

Directions:

1. Melt butter in 12" x 7½" glass baking dish in microwave for 1 minute or until melted.
2. Add salt and pepper. Roll chicken in seasoned butter to coat; arrange in dish. Cover with waxed paper; cook on high 8 minutes.
3. Turn pieces over; top with mushrooms. Cook on high 4–6 minutes.
4. Just before serving, sprinkle with onions and cheeses. Cook on high once more 2–3 minutes, uncovered. Serve over rice. Serves 6.

 This quick dinner was highly rated by adults and children. Since microwaves vary, be sure to check that chicken is done before adding the onions.

Crispy Baked Chicken

Ingredients:

¾ c. flour
1 tsp. salt
¼ tsp. pepper
½ tsp. garlic salt
1½ tsp. paprika
1½ c. cornflakes, crushed
1½ lbs. boneless, skinless chicken breast, or thighs and legs
5 T. butter, divided
6 servings rice

Directions:

1. Preheat oven to 350°.
2. Combine first 6 ingredients; coat chicken with mixture.
3. Melt 3 tablespoons butter in 9" x 13" pan. Add coated chicken to pan.
4. Melt remaining butter and drizzle over chicken.
5. Bake 20–25 minutes, until done. Do not overbake. Serves 4.

 Have your children prepare stuffed celery as an appetizer. You'll need washed and dried celery sticks, plus any or all of the following: peanut butter, cream cheese, cottage cheese, raisins, nuts, sunflower seeds. Have your child fill the celery sticks with cheese, then add toppings as desired. They can arrange them on a plate to serve.

Greek-Style Baked Chicken

Ingredients:

4 boneless, skinless chicken breasts
3–4 tomatoes, diced and drained
2 T. parsley
2 T. fresh mint, chopped
¼ tsp. oregano
⅛ tsp. fresh black pepper
1 red or yellow pepper, diced
8–10 oz. feta cheese, crumbled
1 T. olive oil
4 servings rice or pasta

Directions:

1. Preheat oven to 375°.
2. Coat baking dish with nonstick spray. Arrange chicken in dish; set aside.
3. In bowl combine remaining ingredients; mix well. Spoon over chicken.
4. Bake 25–30 minutes or until firm and opaque. Serve hot; spoon cooking juices and vegetables over each serving. Good served with rice or pasta. Serves 4.

 Feta cheese is a white tangy cheese that adds a fresh, authentic flavor to this dish. Don't substitute another cheese until you've given feta cheese a try. Try adding black olives and/or artichoke hearts for a variation.

Chicken Supreme

Ingredients:

6 boneless chicken breasts
1 pkg. Armour dried beef
6 strips bacon
8 oz. sour cream
1 (10½ oz.) can cream of mushroom soup

Directions:

1. Preheat oven to 275°.
2. Wrap each chicken breast in slices of dried beef. Wrap bacon slice around dried beef. Secure with toothpick. Place in baking dish.
3. Mix sour cream and soup; pour over chicken.
4. Bake 3 hours, covered. Serves 6.

 This results in very moist and tender chicken in a flavorful sauce. Serve with rice or mashed potatoes to take advantage of the sauce. Add steamed broccoli or other colorful vegetable to balance this "pale" entree.

Chicken Breasts in Cream Sauce

Ingredients:

4 chicken breasts, boned, split, and skinned
salt and pepper to taste
¼ lb. butter, melted
1 (10½ oz.) can cream of mushroom soup
1 c. sour cream
1 (6½ oz.) jar mushrooms
½ c. cooking wine or sherry (opt.)

Directions:

1. Preheat oven to 350°.
2. Arrange chicken breasts in greased shallow casserole dish. Season with salt and pepper. Pour melted butter over all.
3. Combine remaining ingredients; spoon over melted butter. Bake uncovered for 1 hour. Serves 4–6.

 This very simple dish is elegant enough for any "company" dinner. If everything is not ready, or the guests are late, you can reduce the oven temperature to low and cover the dish — it will "wait" for you for up to half an hour. You can also easily increase the servings. If you need to serve 8, double the ingredients and bake in a 9" x 13" dish, or larger.

Chicken Casserole

Ingredients:

1 (7 oz.) pkg. small elbow macaroni
½ lb. Velveeta cheese, cubed
1 (10½ oz.) can cream of mushroom soup
2 c. milk
1 c. fresh mushrooms, sliced
4 c. chicken, cooked and cubed
1 (10½ oz.) can cream of chicken soup
1 small jar pimentos (opt.)

Directions:

1. Combine all ingredients. Stir and leave in refrigerator overnight.
2. Bake at 350° for 1 hour. May be prepared same day if the macaroni is cooked before combining it with other ingredients.first. Serves 8–10.

 I thought my pressure cooker was out of steam, so I took off the regulator. Steam shot up like a geyser, soaking the ceiling! The good news is that it washed off the soot from the time the wok caught on fire!

 For a quick and colorful accompaniment try sautéed cherry tomatoes. Heat 1 T. butter and 1 T. olive oil in skillet until sizzling. Add washed and dried (be sure they're dry or oil will splatter) tomatoes to the pan. Shake pan to cover tomatoes in butter. Let them cook, only until warm through. Season with salt, pepper, and a sprinkle of sugar. Add other herbs or Parmesan cheese as desired.

Honey Lemon Chicken

Ingredients:

3 lbs. broiler/fryer chicken (use breasts, thighs, and legs)
salt and pepper to taste
¼ c. vegetable oil
¼ c. honey
2 T. soy sauce
2 T. lemon juice
1 tsp. paprika
¼ tsp. nutmeg
½ tsp. garlic powder
1 egg yolk

Directions:

1. Preheat oven to 350°.
2. Wash chicken; remove skin; pat dry.
3. Place chicken in a large casserole dish; salt and pepper to taste.
4. Mix next 8 ingredients in a bowl; drizzle over chicken.
5. Bake uncovered for 1 hour. Baste occasionally during cooking. Serves 4–6.

 This is a perfect potluck pick! You can easily double or even triple the ingredients to accommodate a large crowd. If you're cooking large amounts, use the right size pan or pans and increase the baking time to be sure the chicken is cooked throughout.

 Serve with hot buttered noodles and steamed broccoli.

Turkey or Chicken Divan

Ingredients:

2 (10 oz.) pkgs. frozen broccoli spears
6 thick slices cooked turkey or 10 slices cooked chicken
¼ c. mayonnaise or salad dressing
1 tsp. lemon juice
1 (10½ oz.) can condensed cream of chicken soup
½ c. dry bread crumbs
1 T. margarine or butter, melted

Directions:

1. Preheat oven to 350°.
2. Cook broccoli as directed on package until almost done; drain.
3. Arrange broccoli in a greased 12" x 8" baking dish. Lay turkey slices on top.
4. In small bowl combine mayonnaise, lemon juice, and soup; pour over turkey.
5. Combine bread crumbs and margarine; sprinkle on top.
6. Bake uncovered 25–30 minutes or until heated through. Serves 4–6.

 This is a tasty way to use leftover turkey or chicken. If you enjoy turkey, remember it's a great family meal not *only* on Thanksgiving. Buy two while they're on sale and put one in the freezer for a special family dinner — or company — on a cold winter night.

Turkey Tetrazzini

Ingredients:

6 oz. vermicelli
1 bunch green onions, chopped
1 lg. green pepper, chopped
6 oz. mushrooms, sliced
1 (2 oz.) jar chopped pimento
2 T. butter
1 (10½ oz.) can mushroom soup
½ tsp. salt
1 c. milk
½ pt. whipping cream
2 c. turkey, cooked and chopped
1 c. grated cheddar cheese

Directions:

1. Preheat oven to 300°.
2. Cook vermicelli according to package directions.
3. Sauté onions, pepper, mushrooms, and pimento in butter.
4. Put vermicelli on bottom of casserole dish.
5. Stir soup, salt, milk, and whipping cream with sautéd vegetables; add turkey. Pour over vermicelli.
6. Bake 1 hour. Sprinkle on cheese. Return to oven 10 minutes or until cheese is melted. Serves 4.

 Here's a good day-after-Thanksgiving dish. Vermicelli is the very thin strand pasta. Its name translates to mean "little worms" (you may or may not want to share that information with your child!).

Turkey Club Deluxe Pizza

Ingredients:

Crust: 1 (10 oz.) can Pillsbury refrigerated all-ready pizza crust
  or your favorite choice for a 12" round
2 tsp. sesame seeds

Topping:

¼ c. reduced calorie mayonnaise
1 tsp. lemon juice
4 oz. (1 cup) shredded Monterey Jack cheese
1 tsp. dried basil leaves
4 oz. deli turkey breast slices, cut into 1" strips
6 slices bacon
1 small tomato, sliced
½ c. shredded Swiss cheese

Directions:

1. Preheat oven to 425°.
2. Prepare crust; sprinkle with sesame seeds. Bake 10–12 minutes.
3. While crust is baking, cook and crumble bacon.
4. Combine lemon juice and mayonnaise in small bowl.
5. Spread lemon and mayonnaise mixture over slightly cooled crust. Top with Monterey Jack cheese, basil, turkey, bacon, and tomatoes. Sprinkle with Swiss cheese.
6. Bake 7–9 minutes or until crust is light brown and cheese is melted. Serves 4–6.

 This recipe will surprise you! It is a big hit with young and old. You can slice it into small squares for an appetizer.

 Quick salads for guests: Cucumbers with dill dressing; cucumbers with red onion slices and vinegar/oil dressing; or apple chunks, celery, nuts, and pineapple chunks with yogurt.

Turkey Patties

Ingredients:

1 lb. ground turkey
⅓ c. bread crumbs
1 egg
¾ tsp. garlic salt
1 T. vegetable oil

Sauce:

1 c. chicken broth
1 T. soy sauce
2 tsp. cornstarch
1 tsp. sugar (opt.)
1 tsp. vinegar
dash white pepper
½ c. each celery, onion,
   green and red pepper,
   tomatoes (whatever you
   have on hand)
4 servings rice

Directions:

1. Mix first 4 ingredients. Form into 4 patties about ¾" thick. Brown in oil in skillet over medium heat; remove patties from pan.
2. Add sauce ingredients to pan; whisk to mix. Add patties, coating them, and simmer until gravy thickens somewhat and turkey is cooked throughout.
3. Add vegetables to pan; cook until tender. Serve with rice. Serves 4.

 Bread crumbs are easy to make if you have a food processor or blender. Drop in a slice or two of day old bread and chop.

 Do not forget to entertain strangers, for by so doing some people have entertained angels without knowing it (Hebrews 13:2).

Really Great Pork Chops

Ingredients:

1 lb. boneless pork chops
salt and pepper to taste
2 T. butter
¼ c. green onion, minced
1 T. mustard
1 (14½ oz.) can chicken broth
2 T. maple syrup
2 T. basalmic vinegar

Directions:

1. Pound pork to flatten. Season meat with salt and pepper.
2. Heat butter in frying pan to medium heat. Sauté pork until done (about 4–5 minutes per side).
3. Remove meat from pan and put it under a "tent" of foil to keep warm.
4. Add onion to pan drippings and sauté for 2 minutes; add mustard and broth. Cook until the liquid is reduced by half.
5. Add maple syrup and basalmic vinegar. Return meat to pan to reheat. Serves 4.

 Serve this delicious meat with mashed potatoes and peas for a great dinner.

 The meat is flattened to make all slices equal in size so they will cook evenly. Let your children help flatten the meat by placing it between two sheets of wax paper and gently flattening it with rolling pin or mallet.

Cajun Chops

Ingredients:

1 T. paprika
1 tsp. seasoned salt
1 tsp. rubbed sage
½ tsp. cayenne pepper
½ tsp. black pepper
½ tsp. garlic powder
4 (½" thick) boneless pork chops
2 T. butter

Directions:

1. Combine seasonings. Coat chops on both sides with mixture.
2. Heat butter over high heat just until it starts to brown (watch carefully).
3. Put chops in pan, reduce heat to medium. Fry on both sides until dark brown, 8–10 minutes. Serves 4.

 Use this mixture of herbs to season fish fillets.

 Pork has been overcooked for decades. Mothers have served "pork chips" in place of pork chops for fear of infecting the family with trichinosis. Scientists have found that trichinae are eliminated at 135°, so cooking pork to 160° (rather than the previously recommended 185°) is safe, and results in a moister and more flavorful meat.

Pork Medallion in Mustard Sauce

Ingredients:

3 T. vegetable oil
1 T. coarse-grained mustard
½ tsp. salt
½ tsp. pepper
2 (12 oz.) pork tenderloins
¼ c. dry white wine

Sauce:

1¾ c. whipping cream
¼ c. coarse grained mustard
¼ tsp. salt
⅓ tsp. white pepper

Directions:

1. Combine first 4 ingredients, stirring well. Rub mixture over pork; place in plastic bag. Refrigerate 8 hours.
2. Place meat on oven rack in a shallow roasting pan. Insert meat thermometer into thickest part of meat. Bake at 375° 25 minutes or until thermometer registers 160°, basting every 10 minutes with wine.
3. Slice meat into ¾" slices. Arrange 4 slices on each dinner plate.
4. Sauce: heat cream on medium or medium low until reduced to 1¼ cup (about 15 minutes). Do *not* boil. Stir in remaining ingredients and heat 1 minute. Spoon over meat. Serves 4.

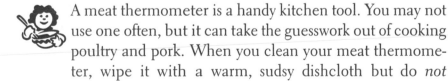 A meat thermometer is a handy kitchen tool. You may not use one often, but it can take the guesswork out of cooking poultry and pork. When you clean your meat thermometer, wipe it with a warm, sudsy dishcloth but do *not* immerse it in water. Store where it won't be broken from bumping against other utensils in a drawer.

Chili Verde

Ingredients:

1½ lbs. boneless pork, cut into 1" cubes
1 medium bell pepper, cut into strips
2 cloves garlic, minced
1 (28 oz.) can diced tomatoes
1 (4 oz.) can diced green chilies
2 T. dried parsley
1 tsp. sugar
1 T. cumin
3 whole cloves
½ c. beef broth
12 flour tortillas
salt and pepper to taste
2 c. Monterey Jack cheese, shredded

Directions:

1. Combine all ingredients except salt, pepper, tortillas, and cheese in a crockpot. Stir well.
2. Cook on low 8–10 hours.
3. Season with salt and pepper. Warm flour tortillas by wrapping six at a time in foil and putting in a 350° oven for 10 minutes.
4. Fill tortillas with chili verde and roll them; add shredded Monterey Jack cheese and pour more chili verde on top. Serves 8.

 If the garlic and green chilies are too spicy for the children, warm a flour tortilla on a griddle or in a skillet and melt grated Monterey Jack cheese on it for a quesadilla. Olé!

Pork Casserole

Ingredients:

3 lbs. lean pork, cut in small cubes
2 medium onions, diced
2 c. celery, chopped
2 c. bell pepper, finely chopped
2 tsp. salt
1 tsp. pepper
1 (8 oz.) pkg. shell macaroni
1 (2 oz.) jar chopped pimentos
1 (4 oz.) can mushroom pieces
1 (10½ oz.) can cream of mushroom soup
1 (10½ oz.) can cream of chicken soup
⅓ c. soy sauce
1 (3 oz.) can chow mein noodles

Directions:

1. Preheat oven to 300°.
2. Brown meat with onions, celery, and peppers in small roasting pan, using a small amount of butter if necessary. Season with salt and pepper.
3. Cook macaroni 8 minutes; drain well and add to cooked ingredients.
4. Blend mixture together with soups and soy sauce. Bake 1 hour.
5. Sprinkle top generously with chow mein noodles. Heat 5 minutes longer and serve. Serves 10.

 Roasting vegetables and pork together eliminates a messy top of the stove and brings out the natural sweetness of the vegetables.

Grilled Salmon

Ingredients:

2 salmon fillets (about 1 lb. each)
½ c. vegetable oil
½ c. lemon juice
4 green onions, thinly sliced
3 T. fresh minced parsley
1½ tsp. fresh minced rosemary or ½ tsp. dried rosemary
½ tsp. salt
⅓ tsp. pepper

Directions:

1. Place salmon in shallow dish. Combine remaining ingredients and mix well. Set aside ¼ cup for basting; pour the rest over the salmon. Cover and refrigerate all for 30 minutes.
2. Drain; discard marinade.
3. Grill salmon over medium coals, skin side down, 15–20 minutes or until fish flakes easily. Baste occasionally with reserved marinade. Serves 4.

 Seafood is terrific on the grill and a welcome change from hamburgers. Baste the fish frequently so it does not dry out. Do not overcook.

White Manhattan Clam Linguine

Ingredients:

2 (6½ oz.) cans clams, drained (reserve liquid)
3 qts. water
1 tsp. salt
8 oz. linguine
4 T. margarine or butter, divided
2 T. parsley
1 T. fresh or ½ tsp. dried basil
¾ tsp. thyme
3 cloves garlic, chopped
½ c. whipping cream
½ c. dry white wine or cooking sherry
¼ c. Parmesan cheese

Directions:

1. Heat reserved clam liquid, water, and salt to boiling. Add linguine and boil 8–10 minutes, until just tender; drain. Return linguine to pot and toss with 2 tablespoons margarine.
2. Heat 2 tablespoons margarine, parsley, basil, thyme, garlic, and clams until heated through. Stir in whipping cream and wine until heated through.
3. Pour sauce over linguine; add Parmesan cheese and toss. Serve with garlic bread and tossed salad. Serves 4.

 Take the grease off soup or gravy by "mopping" it up with a lettuce leaf. Swishing the lettuce leaf over the top will collect the offending grease.

Oven "Fried" Fish

Ingredients:

¼ lb. butter or margarine
8 fish fillets (1 ½ lb. any white fish)
2 eggs, well beaten
2 c. fine bread crumbs
salt and pepper to taste

Directions:

1. Preheat oven to 375°.
2. Place butter in 9" x 13" pan and put in oven. Melt butter — watch carefully so that it doesn't burn.
3. Remove from oven.
4. Dip fish fillets in egg, then crumbs to coat on both sides. Season with salt and pepper and place in buttered pan, turning once to coat on both sides.
5. Bake 15–20 minutes. Serves 4–6.

 Go fishing. Make a fishing pole by tying a length of string to the end of a dowel, paper towel tube, or even chopstick. Make a hook using a pipe cleaner, bent paper clip, or cardboard cut to resemble a hook. Make fish out of paper — any size, any color (try paper bags, newspaper, construction paper, or junk mail). Cut a large hole in fish to assure good fishing. Your child can fish while you cook dinner.

Orange Roughy Parmesan

Ingredients:

2 lbs. orange roughy
2 T. lemon juice
½ c. Parmesan cheese
4 T. margarine or butter, softened
3 T. mayonnaise
3 T. green onion, chopped
¼ tsp. salt
pepper to taste
dash Tabasco sauce

Directions:

1. In greased baking dish arrange fish in single layer.
2. Brush with lemon juice; let stand 10 minutes.
3. In a small bowl combine remaining ingredients.
4. Broil fish under preheated broiler 5 minutes.
5. Spread with cheese mixture and broil additional 2–3 minutes. Watch closely so that it doesn't burn. Serves 4.

 This dish is elegant enough for company. Since it requires last-minute preparation, have the rest of your menu either be done ahead and in the refrigerator or waiting for you patiently on the stove. Don't plan on doing six last-minute preparations — you'll be a nervous wreck!

 After using a lemon, store the remaining part of the lemon in the freezer. Cut it into quarters and you'll always have lemon ready to use.

Manicotti in Minutes

Ingredients:

1 (32 oz.) jar spaghetti sauce

1 (16 oz.) can diced tomatoes, undrained

1 clove garlic, minced or ½ tsp. dried minced garlic

2 c. low-fat cottage cheese

1 c. low-fat ricotta cheese

2 egg whites

4 T. fresh parsley, chopped

8 oz. (14) manicotti shells uncooked

1 c. water

Directions:

1. Preheat oven to 350°.
2. Combine spaghetti sauce, tomatoes, and garlic; set aside.
3. Combine cheeses, egg whites, and parsley. Stuff shells with cheese mixture, using a small spatula or better yet a pastry bag.
4. Fill bottom of 9" x 13" pan with 2 cups tomato mixture. Arrange stuffed shells in single layer over sauce; cover shells with remaining 3 cups sauce.
5. Pour water evenly over top. (Don't be concerned about the watery appearance; it will be absorbed during the cooking process.)
6. Cover dish with foil and bake 50 minutes. Remove foil and bake another 10 minutes. Serves 8.

 Have your child draw a picture or write a message on a small piece of paper. Roll the paper and stick it into a piece of uncooked manicotti. The child can give the secret message to a sibling, dad, or neighbor.

Vegetarian Pizza

Ingredients:

¾ c. Pesto sauce
¾ c. spaghetti sauce
1 c. grated cheese, any kind
1 carrot, peeled and grated
1 stalk broccoli florets, cut in bite-sized pieces
½ c. black olives, sliced
½ c. feta cheese
1 pizza round or crust, store-bought or homemade

Directions:

1. Preheat oven to 400°.
2. Spread pesto sauce on pizza round; spread spaghetti sauce over pesto sauce.
3. Sprinkle on the cheese; then carrot and broccoli.
4. Top with olives and feta cheese.
5. Bake 10 minutes. Serves 6.

 "Build your own pizza" can be an easy, informal party idea. Provide the base rounds in individual sizes and have guests bring an assortment of toppings. Several individual-sized pizzas can bake at a time.

 You can buy fresh pizza crust dough from many bakeries, pizza places, and grocery stores. Ask around.

Crockpot Vegetable Pasta

Ingredients:

2 T. butter
2 small zucchini, peeled and thinly sliced
1½ c. fresh mushrooms, sliced
1 (10 oz.) pkg. frozen chopped broccoli, thawed
2 carrots, peeled and thinly sliced
4 green onions, sliced
1 clove garlic, minced
½ tsp. basil
½ tsp. salt
¼ tsp. pepper
1 c. grated Parmesan cheese
12 oz. fettuccine
1 c. shredded mozzarella cheese
1 c. whipping cream
2 egg yolks

Directions:

1. Rub walls of crockpot with butter. Place zucchini, mushrooms, broccoli, carrots, onions, garlic, seasonings, and Parmesan cheese in crockpot.
2. Cover and cook on high 2 hours or until vegetables are tender.
3. Cook fettuccine according to package directions; drain.
4. To the crockpot add cooked fettuccine, mozzarella cheese, cream, and egg yolks; stir to blend well.
5. Allow to heat on high 10–15 minutes before serving. Will stay warm on low for up to 30 minutes. Serves 8.

 To clean mushrooms, wipe them with a damp paper towel. Don't immerse them in water because they absorb too much liquid. If possible, buy mushrooms with closed caps, without the gills showing.

Stuffed Shells

Ingredients:

12 jumbo pasta shells

1 tsp. minced garlic

¼ c. mushrooms, diced

¼ c. onion, chopped

¼ c. zucchini, chopped

¼ c. red bell pepper, chopped

2 T. olive oil

1 tsp. nutmeg

1 T. grated Parmesan cheese

2 c. spinach, cooked and chopped

1 egg, beaten

4 T. ricotta cheese

2 c. tomato sauce or favorite spaghetti sauce

1 c. mozzarella cheese, shredded

Directions:

1. Preheat oven to 350°.
2. Cook pasta shells according to package directions; drain.
3. Sauté garlic and vegetables in olive oil. Add nutmeg and Parmesan cheese.
4. Cool and stir in spinach and egg. Blend in ricotta cheese.
5. Stuff shells and arrange on bed of tomato sauce in a 9" x 13" baking dish.
6. Bake 10 minutes; top with mozzarella cheese. Bake 5 more minutes. Serves 6.

 Make your own baby food and freeze it in disposable bottle liners. Measure the food into the bag as it lines the bottle, twist tie the top and freeze. This is a sanitary way to store individual portions. To use, dip bag in warm water, slip food out and heat.

You can also freeze homemade baby food in ice cube trays. Pop out the "food cubes" when they're frozen and store several in a freezer bag.

Chili Relleno Casserole

Ingredients:

1 (5 oz.) can evaporated milk
3 T. flour
½ tsp. salt
2 eggs, separated
1 (4 oz.) can whole green chilies
1 lb. cheddar cheese
1 lb. Monterey Jack cheese
1 (8 oz.) can tomato sauce

Directions:

1. Preheat oven to 350°.
2. Grease casserole dish.
3. Mix together milk, flour, salt, and egg yolks. Beat egg whites; fold into milk mixture.
4. Rinse seeds from green chilies. Open flat and layer on bottom of casserole dish. Layer cheddar and Monterey Jack cheeses. Repeat. Pour liquid over layers. Serves 4–6.
5. Bake 40–45 minutes. Pour tomato sauce on top; bake 15 minutes more.

 To help a young child to take distasteful medicine, run an ice cube over his tongue. This will temporarily freeze the taste buds.

Bean Burritos

Ingredients:

1 small onion, chopped
3 (15¼ oz.) cans red kidney beans
1 (6 oz.) can tomato paste
⅓ c. water
2 T. brown sugar
1 T. cider vinegar
3 cloves garlic, minced
2 T. chili powder
salt to taste
1 pkg. (9") flour tortillas

Directions:

1. In frying pan bring small amount of water to boil. Add onions; cook until tender.
2. Add beans, tomato paste, and ⅓ cup water; cook until blended.
3. Add sugar, vinegar, and spices; cook over medium heat 15 minutes.
4. Warm tortillas; place a spoon of bean mixture down the middle of each. Fold in half; then roll up.
5. Serve with shredded cheddar, sour cream, salsa, or guacamole. Serves 6–8.

 An "old wives' tale" says that adding ¼ teaspoon or so of ginger to a recipe with beans will reduce the potential gas problem.

 For a variation on this recipe, try substituting black beans for kidney beans. Add cumin for a different flavor.

Vegetarian Chili

Ingredients:

1 medium onion, chopped
2 T. vegetable oil
minced garlic to taste
1 (48 oz.) can V–8 juice
2 (16 oz.) cans of your favorite beans, drained (black, red, kidney, Great Northern, or mixed)
1 tsp. Worcestershire sauce
1 tsp. sugar
1 tsp. salt
2 T. chili powder

Directions:

1. Sauté onion in oil until transparent. Add minced garlic; cook 1 minute.
2. Add remaining ingredients; heat gently to simmer.
3. Reduce heat and simmer several hours to thicken. Serves 4.

 Try this chili in a crockpot. You can leave it simmering without worrying about it burning.

 Explore a fresh fruit and vegetable market with your child in the summertime. When you return, let your child create a centerpiece of fresh fruits and vegetables while you make fresh salsa.

Best-Ever Meatloaf

Ingredients:

2 eggs
⅔ c. milk
3 slices bread, torn in pieces
½ c. onion, chopped
½ c. carrot, grated
1 c. cheddar or Mozzarella
   cheese, shredded
1 T. fresh or 1 tsp. dried
   parsley

1 tsp. basil
1 tsp. salt
I tsp. pepper
1½ lbs. ground beef

Topping:

½ c. tomato sauce
½ c. brown sugar
1 tsp. dry mustard

Directions:

1. Preheat oven to 350°.
2. In large bowl beat eggs. Add milk and bread; let stand until liquid is absorbed.
3. Stir in onion, carrots, cheese, and seasonings. Add beef; mix well (using hands to mix).
4. In a shallow baking pan shape mixture into 7" x 3" x 2" loaf. Bake 45 minutes.
5. Meanwhile, combine topping ingredients. Spoon some over meatloaf. Bake 30 minutes longer, occasionally adding topping. Let stand 10 minutes before serving. Serves 6.

 You can substitute 1 cup of crushed saltine crackers for the bread in this recipe; it lends a slightly different texture and flavor.

 Wash and dry the Styrofoam tray from the meat. On a cutting board cut slits in the bottom of the tray, about 1" apart. Cut strips of paper about 1" wide. Weave the strips through the tray; secure ends with tape.

Meatloaf Mexicali

Ingredients:

1 ½ lb. lean ground beef
¾ c. prepared tomato salsa
1 egg
12 Ritz or Townhouse crackers, crushed
6 oz. cheddar cheese, grated

Directions:

1. Preheat oven to 350°.
2. In large bowl combine meat, salsa, egg, crackers. Add half the cheese.
3. In shallow baking pan form ground beef mixture into a 9" x 5" loaf. Bake 1 hour and 10 minutes.
4. Meanwhile, sprinkle remaining cheese on top and place on top during last 2 minutes of baking. Serves 6.

Here's a change of taste for meatloaf. Try Spanish rice as a side dish as well as warm, buttered flour tortillas folded into quarters.

Make Mexico the topic for dinner conversation. Read about the country and the customs. Share what you've learned at dinner.

Salisbury Steak

Ingredients:

1 (10¾ oz.) can golden mushroom soup, divided
1½ lb. ground beef
½ c. dry bread crumbs
½ tsp. salt
⅛ tsp. pepper
1 onion, finely chopped
1 egg, slightly beaten
⅓ c. water

Directions:

1. Preheat oven to 350°.
2. Combine half the soup with next six ingredients and mix well; shape into oval-shaped patties.
3. Arrange patties in 9" x 13" pan and bake uncovered 30 minutes. Skim off fat.
4. In small bowl combine remaining soup and water and spoon over patties.
5. Return to oven and bake 10 more minutes. Serves 6.

 This will become a family favorite. It is simple, low mess, and delicious. Bake potatoes in the oven at the same time. (You may need to start the potatoes 15 minutes before you put the meat in.) For baked potatoes, pierce the potatoes with a fork before baking and about halfway through the cooking time. When the moisture is released you end up with a fluffy, light texture rather than a heavier texture.

Quick and Easy Microwave Meatloaf

Ingredients:

½ c. milk
1 lb. ground beef or any
   ground meat
1 c. Quaker oats
¼ c. ketchup
1 tsp. salt
2 T. Worcestershire sauce

½ tsp. pepper
¼ tsp. garlic powder
1 egg
½ c. ketchup
2 T. brown sugar
2 T. sugar
1 tsp. prepared mustard

Directions:

1. Combine milk, meat, oats, ketchup, salt, Worcestershire sauce, pepper, garlic powder, and egg. Place in 2-quart round casserole dish.
2. Form into a ring. Put juice glass upside down in center. Microwave on high 14 minutes.
3. Mix remaining ingredients together; spread on top. Microwave an additional 5 minutes. Serves 6.

 Put an apron on your child and seat him at the table with a large bowl. As you measure in the ingredients let him squish them all together with his hands. Let him form the ring. You can bet he'll eat *this* meatloaf!

 Meatloaf sandwiches are a good way to use leftover meatloaf.

Swedish Meatballs

Ingredients:

1 ½ lbs. lean ground beef
½ c. bread crumbs
1 egg
salt and pepper to taste
¼ c. Parmesan cheese
4–5 T. ketchup
1 tsp. Worcestershire sauce
2 (10½ oz.) cans beef consomme soup
2 T. flour

Directions:

1. Mix together all except soup and flour. Roll into small balls and brown in skillet or on baking sheet under broiler. Place meatballs in saucepan.
2. Mix flour with soup and ½ soup can water. Stir and simmer with meatballs in pan for ½ hour. Serve over noodles or mashed potatoes. Serves 6.

 Make this Sweden night! Draw Swedish flags for decorations. Find out all you can about Sweden.

 But no stranger had to spend the night in the street, for my door was always open to the traveler (Job 31:32).

Homespun Meat Pie

Ingredients:

2 large red potatoes
1 lb. ground beef
4 oz. can of mushrooms,
   drained
1 egg
⅓ c. onion, chopped
¼ c. dry bread crumbs

1 ¼ tsp. salt, divided
dash pepper
3 T. milk
¼ lb. Velveeta cheese,
   cubed
1 T. parsley, chopped

Directions:

1. Preheat oven to 400°.
2. Peel potatoes. Cut them in eighths and cover with water in a saucepan; boil until tender.
3. Combine meat, mushrooms, egg, onion, bread crumbs, 1 tsp. salt, and pepper; mix lightly.
4. Treat a 9" pie plate with non-stick spray. Press meat mixture onto bottom and sides of the pie plate.
5. Bake 15 minutes. Mash hot potatoes with milk; stir in cheese, parsley, and ¼ tsp. salt.
6. Remove meat shell from oven; reduce oven temperature to 350°. Drain meat shell; fill with potato mixture. Return to oven; continue baking 10 minutes. Serves 6.

 This is a great way to use leftover baked potatoes. When you prepare baked potatoes, cook one or two extra. Use them for Homespun Meat Pie or a breakfast of diced, cooked potatoes fried with chopped onion and diced bacon.

Cheese 'n' Sausage Calzones

Ingredients:

1 (15 oz.) container of ricotta cheese

½ lb. (2 c.) shredded Mozzarella cheese

½ c. grated Parmesan cheese

1 tsp. oregano

1 tsp. basil

½ c. onion, finely chopped

½ c. green pepper, finely chopped

1 clove garlic, minced

1 T. cooking oil

1 lb. bulk Italian sausage

5 loaves (1 lb. each) frozen bread dough, thawed

¼ c. butter, melted

1 (16 oz.) jar spaghetti sauce, heated

Directions:

1. Preheat oven to 350°.
2. Combine cheeses, oregano, and basil; set aside.
3. Sauté onion, green pepper, and garlic in oil until tender; add to cheese mixture.
4. In same skillet brown sausage; drain and stir into cheese mixture.
5. Divide each loaf of dough into 4 portions (or 8 smaller portions); roll each into a circle 6" across.
6. Spoon filling on half of each circle; fold dough over filling and seal edges. Repeat with remaining dough and filling.
7. Brush with butter; place on greased baking sheet.
8. Bake 25 minutes or until golden. Serve with spaghetti sauce for dipping.

 This is a party recipe. You'll have 20–40 calzones, depending on the size you choose. If you wish, you can freeze some of the calzones after baking.

Marinated Flank Steak

Ingredients:

1½–2 lbs. flank steak
1 c. red wine, or ¾ c. water and ¼ c. wine vinegar
½ c. oil
½ c. soy sauce
1 tsp. garlic powder
½ tsp. powdered ginger
¼ tsp. black pepper

Directions:

1. Place meat in a large casserole dish. Mix remaining ingredients and pour on top.
2. Poke meat repeatedly with a fork to tenderize and allow marinade to soak in. Turn over and make sure to let each side get well-soaked. Marinate for at least 1 hour.
3. Broil or grill for 7–8 minutes on each side. Slice flank steak on the diagonal. Serve with parsleyed potatoes and green beans. Serves 4.

 Transfer this to a large freezer-strength plastic bag and keep in the freezer. As the meat thaws, it marinades. When thawed, discard marinade and broil or grill.

 Apply sweet-based sauces to the meat during the last 10 minutes of cooking on the grill, to avoid burning due to the sugar in the sauce.

Barbe Cups

Ingredients:

12 oz. ground beef, browned and drained
½ c. barbecue sauce
1 T. minced onion
2 T. brown sugar
10 biscuits, in tubes or homemade
1 c. shredded cheddar cheese

Directions:

1. Preheat oven to 400°.
2. Add sauce, onion, and brown sugar to meat. Line muffin tins with biscuits. Spoon in meat mixture and top with cheese. Bake 10–12 minutes. Makes 10.

 When ground beef is on sale, stock up! Brown the beef in batches; drain on paper towels to remove excess grease. Measure into freezer-strength plastic containers or bags. If you keep frozen beef on hand, this recipe will be even easier to have ready for a quick, delicious dinner or lunch.

 I dropped a large, full bottle of barbecue sauce. It broke and sprayed sauce all over my kitchen and dining room walls and ceiling. My family laughed; I cried. I thought I'd never get it cleaned up.

Slow Simmering BBQ Sandwiches

Ingredients:

One 3-lb. beef brisket
½ c. water
3 T. white vinegar
2 T. Worcestershire sauce
1 tsp. ground cumin or chili powder
1 c. bottled barbeque sauce

Directions:

1. Cut the meat, if necessary, to fit crockpot. Mix together water, vinegar, Worcestershire sauce, cumin or chili powder; pour over meat in cooker. Cover and cook on low 10–12 hours or on high 4–5 hours.
2. About 1 hour before serving, remove meat from cooker and cool to touch. Shred meat (easiest if done with fingers!) and discard fat.
3. Discard liquid from crockpot. Set crockpot on high and return shredded meat to crockpot; stir in barbecue sauce. Cover and cook for 30–45 minutes or until heated through.
4. Serve on buns with pickles or onions to taste. Serves 10.

 Here is a good informal company dish for a day when you will be busy before the company arrives. Let your company help by bringing a salad or dessert.

Jewish Baked Beans

Ingredients:

1 ½ lb. ground beef, ground turkey, or sausage
1 large onion, chopped
2 (15 oz.) cans Great northern beans, drained
1 (27 oz.) can kidney beans, drained
1 (15 oz.) can butter beans, drained
1 (18 oz.) Kraft Honey barbecue sauce
1 T. prepared mustard
¾ c. brown sugar
garlic to taste

Directions:

Brown meat and onion together and drain. Mix with other ingredients. Cook in crockpot 4–6 hours on low or put in 9" x 13" pan and bake at 350° for 1 ½ hours.

 This dish travels well in the crockpot and can stay warm until you're ready to serve.

 Talk about the different types of beans in this recipe. If you use dried beans instead of canned beans, have your child do this craft while you're soaking the beans or cooking. Place different beans in the cups of a muffin tin. On a piece of cardboard (those from the laundry work well here), have your child draw a design or even a simple shape. Using white glue, let the child fill in the design with the different colored beans.

Beef Rouladen

Ingredients:

½ c. Dijon mustard
2 lb. (approx.) top round or
    flank steak cut in 8 pieces,
    each about ¼" thick and
    3–4" across
salt and pepper to taste
8 bacon strips

1 large onion, cut in thin
    wedges
3 T. cooking oil
3 c. beef broth
⅓ c. flour
½ c. water
chopped fresh parsley (opt.)

Directions:

1. Lightly spread mustard on each slice of steak; sprinkle with salt and pepper.
2. Place one bacon strip, lengthwise, and a few onion wedges on each slice. Roll up and secure with toothpicks.
3. Brown in skillet in oil; drain.
4. Add broth and bring to a boil. Reduce heat; cover and simmer 1½ hours or until meat is tender. Remove meat and keep warm.
5. Combine flour and water until smooth; gradually stir into broth. Bring to boil, stirring constantly until thick and bubbly.
6. Remove toothpicks and return the beef roll to gravy. Heat through. Sprinkle with parsley. Serves 8.

 I used to sell knives (for only one summer). In a lady's home I demonstrated how efficient her kitchen could be using the "World's Finest Knives." I assured her that a sharper knife is a safer knife. I sliced my finger with a knife and the woman ended up driving me to an urgent care center, where I required surgery to repair my finger. She did *not* buy any knives.

 This meat dish is from Germany. Have your children learn about Germany today. Tell about what you've learned at dinner.

Mexican Lasagna

Ingredients:

1 lb. ground beef or turkey
1 pkg. dry taco mix seasoning
1 c. water
12 (6") corn tortillas
1 c. salsa
1 (8 oz.) can tomato sauce
1 (15 oz.) can whole kernel corn, drained
1 (4 oz.) can sliced black olives, drained
1 (4 oz.) can mild chilies, drained
2 c. shredded Monterey Jack cheese

Directions:

1. Preheat oven to 375°.
2. Brown meat; add seasoning and 1 cup water. Cook until thick.
3. Spray 9" x 13" pan with cooking spray. Place 6 tortillas on bottom of pan, overlapping them.
4. Mix salsa and tomato sauce; set aside.
5. Top tortillas with half the meat, corn, olives, and chilies.
6. Pour half the salsa and sauce mixture over this and sprinkle with 1 cup Monterey Jack cheese. Repeat, finishing with cheese. Bake 30 minutes. Serves 6–8.

 The ingredients for Mexican Lasagna can be easily kept on hand in the pantry and freezer for a spur of the moment fiesta!

 Serve pineapple with chili or other spicy foods; it tastes good and helps aid good digestion.

Sherried Beef

Ingredients:

3 lbs. stew meat
3 (10½ oz) cans cream of mushroom soup
⅓ c. sherry or cooking wine
1 envelope dry onion soup mix
pepper to taste
6 servings noodles

Directions:

Combine all ingredients except noodles and bake in Dutch oven at 350° for 3 hours, or cook in crockpot on low 8–10 hours. Serves 6.

 Serve Sherried Beef over noodles with steamed vegetables and Italian bread!

 Thank God for dirty dishes
They have a tale to tell.
While other folks go hungry,
We're eating very well.
With home and health
and happiness,
We surely shouldn't fuss,
For by this stack of evidence,
God's been good to us!
         —Author unknown

Friendship Casserole

Ingredients:

2 lbs. ground beef
1 (48 oz.) jar spaghetti sauce
2 T. sugar
1 (1 lb.) pkg. medium egg noodles
½ c. margarine or butter
¾ tsp. onion salt
¾ tsp. garlic salt
½ c. grated Parmesan cheese
12 oz. shredded mozzarella cheese

Directions:

1. Preheat oven to 350°.
2. Brown meat; drain fat.
3. Add spaghetti sauce and sugar to meat; simmer 20 minutes.
4. Cook noodles as directed; drain and toss with margarine, salts, and Parmesan cheese.
5. Treat to 9" x 13" pans with nonstick spray. In both pans layer half the sauce, all the noodles, rest of sauce; top with mozzarella cheese.
6. Cover with foil; bake 45 minutes. Serves 16.

 Since this recipe makes enough for two casseroles, plan one for your family and one for a friend. Think of someone who might need a reminder that they have friends who care about them — a new mom in your neighborhood, a family who's moving, someone with an illness.

Spaghetti Pie

Ingredients:

4 oz. spaghetti

1 T. margarine or butter

1 egg, beaten

¼ c. grated Parmesan
   cheese

½ lb. lean ground beef

½ c. onion, chopped

½ c. green pepper, chopped

2 cloves garlic, minced

½ tsp. fennel seed

1 (8 oz.) can tomato sauce

1 tsp. dried oregano

1 c. lowfat cottage cheese

½ c. shredded mozzarella
   cheese

Directions:

1. Preheat oven to 350°.
2. Cook pasta according to directions; drain well. Return to saucepan; stir margarine or butter into pasta until melted.
3. Stir in egg and Parmesan cheese.
4. Spray 9" pie plate with nonstick cooking spray. Press spaghetti onto bottom and up sides of plate, forming a crust.
5. Cook beef, onion, green pepper, garlic, and fennel seed in saucepan until onion is tender and meat is no longer pink; drain fat.
6. Stir in tomato sauce and oregano; heat through.
7. Spread cottage cheese on bottom and up sides of crust. Spread meat mixture over cottage cheese; sprinkle mozzarella cheese over meat mixture. Bake uncovered 20–25 minutes. Let stand 5 minutes and cut into wedges to serve. Serves 6.

 It's important not to overcook pasta, or you'll end up with a pound of glue. "Al dente" means "to the bite." Cook pasta until it is slightly firm to the bite. A time-honored tradition for testing pasta is to pull a strand from the pot and juggle it back and forth in your hands until it's cool enough to taste. If it "bites" back slightly, it's done. If the recipe requires mixing pasta with additional ingredients and additional cooking, undercook pasta to be safe.

 This is a very easy recipe to double. The pie freezes well, or makes a good gift for another family.

Sirloin Pummerville

Ingredients:

1 (12 oz) bag wide egg noodles
1½ lb. ground sirloin, or very lean beef
1½ T. butter or margarine
3 (8 oz.) cans tomato sauce
1 c. cottage cheese
8 oz. cream cheese
1 c. sour cream
¾ c. green onions, diced
¾ c. bell pepper, diced

Directions:

1. Preheat oven to 350°.
2. Boil noodles and drain; add butter or margarine.
3. Brown meat; drain. Add tomato sauce.
4. Mix cottage cheese, cream cheese, and sour cream; stir in diced onions and bell pepper.
5. In 9" x 13" glass dish layer noodles, cheese mixture, and meat; repeat layers.
6. Cook 30 minutes. Serves 12.

 Sirloin may be too expensive to use every time, but it is a flavorful addition when the budget allows or when it is on special.

 When cooking the noodles, undercook them slightly, drain them in a colander, and rinse them quickly with cold water. This will stop the cooking process immediately. Place the noodles in a bowl and add butter, margarine, or olive oil. The butter will help prevent the noodles from sticking and turning into one large clump!

"Sort of" Lasagna

Ingredients:

1 medium yellow onion
2 T. butter or margarine
1 lb. ground beef
1 tsp. garlic powder
3 (14 oz.) cans diced tomatoes
2 (14 oz.) cans tomato sauce
1 tsp. oregano
2 c. (8 oz.) mozzarella cheese
2 c. (8 oz.) colby cheese
2 c. (8 oz.) Monterey Jack cheese
6–9 pieces of lasagna pasta

Directions:

1. Preheat oven to 375°.
2. Dice onion; sauté in butter or margarine until just beginning to brown.
3. Add ground beef and garlic powder; brown. In large saucepan combine tomatoes, tomato sauce, and oregano; begin simmering. Add ground beef. Simmer at least ten minutes — an hour is even better!
4. Cook pasta according to package directions; drain.
5. In 9" x 13" baking dish layer sauce, some of each cheese, pasta. Repeat, finishing with sauce and cheese. Bake 40 minutes. Serves 12.

Serve a tossed salad with your lasagna, and put a helper in charge of washing and tearing the lettuce.

Crockpot Chili

Ingredients:

1 (15 oz.) can pinto beans, drained
1 (15 oz.) can kidney beans, drained
1 (15 oz.) can chili beans, drained
2 lbs. ground beef, browned
2–2½ tsp. chili powder
1 tsp. cumin
2 (15 oz.) cans diced tomatoes
salt to taste
garnish with shredded Monterey Jack and cheddar cheeses,
    avocado slices, and diced onion

Directions:

1. Brown ground beef in skillet; drain.
2. Mix everything together in crockpot. Heat on low 8–10 hours.
3. Serve with shredded Monterey Jack and cheddar cheeses, avocado slices, onions. Serves 6–8.

 Crockpot meals are a God-send on those days when work or carpooling occupies the late afternoon. Spread leftover chili on hot dogs in buns for chili dogs.

Sloppy Joes

Ingredients:

1½–2 lbs. lean hamburger
1 T. dried onion flakes
1 pkg. sloppy joe mix
1 (15 oz.) can tomato sauce
1 (10½ oz.) can chicken gumbo soup
½ cup grated cheddar cheese
6 hamburger buns

Directions:

1. Brown hamburger and onion; drain excess fat.
2. Chop meat very small. Add remaining ingredients except cheese to meat; simmer 30 minutes or longer.
3. Top with cheese and serve on buns. Serves 6.

 This sounds a little unusual, but it's a tested winner. Serve from a crockpot and it will stay warm and ready for hours.

Tator-Tot Casserole

Ingredients:

1½ lbs. ground beef
2 cans mixed vegetables, drained, or 1 (16 oz.) pkg. frozen
    mixed vegetables, thawed
1 (10½ oz.) can cream of mushroom or cream of celery soup
1 c. milk
1 can Durkee fried onions
1 (32 oz.) pkg. frozen tater tots

Directions:

1.　Preheat oven to 350°.
2.　Cook and drain ground beef; place in bottom of 9" x 13" glass dish.
3.　Spread mixed vegetables over beef.
4.　Mix soup and milk; spread over vegetables.
5.　Sprinkle on onions and top with one layer of tater tots. Bake 45 minutes. Serves 7–8.

 These meat and potato casseroles are family pleasers. A green salad dessert completes this easy meal.

 Play the "What's missing" game with your child. Draw pictures of familiar items (house, face, car, boat). Leave out a few essentials (no eyes, no wheels, no door). Ask your child to identify or draw in the missing part. This is a good "waiting quietly in the restaurant" game.

Gorge of

DESSERTS

Best Ever Cookies

Ingredients:

1 c. brown sugar, firmly packed	3 c. flour
1 c. sugar	1½ c. oats
¾ c. vegetable oil	1 tsp. cream of tartar
1 c. butter, softened	2 c. Rice Krispies
1 egg	1 c. chocolate chips
1 tsp. vanilla	1 c. butterscotch chips
	1 c. coconut

Directions:

1. Preheat oven to 350°.
2. Cream sugars, oil, and butter.
3. Add egg and vanilla; mix in flour, oats, cream of tartar, and Rice Krispies.
4. Stir in chips and coconut; roll into balls.
5. Bake on ungreased cookie sheets 8–10 minutes.

 To entertain your children, try the following crafts with an empty oatmeal box.

Car Tunnel: With scissors or exacto-knife cut off bottom and top of oatmeal box. Cut box in half lengthwise. Cover outside of box half with brown paper. Decorate with crayons and turn upside down for a tunnel.

Mailbox: Cover box with paper, decorate if desired. Cut slot in side of box for letters. Write name of child on box. Write "U.S. Mail" on lid and send love notes to your child.

Drum: Cut box down to 6½"–7" in length. Cover box with gift wrap or construction paper. Tape in place. Punch two holes in sides near end of box. Thread ribbon through holes (measure length to go from one side of drum up in back of child's neck down to other side of drum). Knot ribbon on inside. Use spoons for drumsticks.

Aggression Cookies

Ingredients:

- 1 c. brown sugar
- 2 c. oatmeal
- 1 c. flour
- ⅔ c. margarine or butter
- 2 tsp. baking soda

Directions:

1. Preheat oven to 350°.
2. Place all ingredients into bowl. Knead and play with this dough as long as you wish. The longer the dough is worked, the better the cookies are.
3. Drop heaping teaspoons of dough onto ungreased cookie sheet; bake 12 minutes. Makes 2 dozen cookies.

 This cookie is a little like an oatmeal shortbread. It is an excellent choice for little boys and girls who are learning how to bake.

 Try this cooking adventure when siblings are squabbling. The energy they expend annoying each other can be poured into kneading the dough — and the end result will be sweeter for everyone.

Chocolate Chip Peanut Butter Cookies

Ingredients:

½ c. (1 stick) butter, softened
½ c. shortening
1 c. creamy peanut butter
1 c. granulated sugar
1 c. brown sugar, packed
2 eggs

2½ c. flour
1½ tsp. baking soda
1 tsp. baking powder
½ tsp. salt
2 c. semisweet chocolate
    chips

Directions:

1. Preheat oven to 375°.
2. In large bowl beat butter, shortening, peanut butter, sugars, and eggs on medium speed until well blended.
3. Stir together flour, baking soda, baking powder, and salt. Add to butter mixture, beating until well blended.
4. Stir in chips; drop by rounded teaspoons onto ungreased cookie sheet.
5. Bake 8–10 minutes or until set. Cool slightly; remove to wire rack. Makes about 6 dozen cookies.

 If you're baking at high altitude (over 3,000 feet), reduce baking powder and baking soda by 25 percent. Reduce granulated (white) sugar by 2 tablespoons per cup. Measure brown sugar, without firmly packing it, and it will be about right. Because high altitude is usually a drier climate you may need to add a teaspoon or two of water to the flour to reach the right dough consistency. These basic rules work pretty well with most baked goods. But remember: practice makes perfect.

Double Chocolate Chip Cookies

Ingredients:

1 c. margarine or butter
1½ c. brown sugar
2 eggs
2 tsp. vanilla
½ tsp. salt
⅔ c. cocoa
2½ c. flour
¾ tsp. baking soda
2 c. chocolate chips

Directions:

1. Preheat oven to 350°.
2. Cream butter; add brown sugar and eggs. Mix in vanilla, salt, and cocoa.
3. Stir in flour and baking soda. Add chocolate chips.
4. Bake 8–10 minutes. Cool 1 minute before taking from cookie sheet. Makes 5 dozen.

 One mom's comfort food: "Chocolate chips have been special since I snuck them out of the bottom drawer growing up at home."

 Seen on a refrigerator: "Last week my house was clean, the wash was done, the dishes washed ... too bad you missed it."

Molasses Cookies

Ingredients:

¾ c. shortening (6 T. Crisco and 6 T. butter works best)
1 c. brown sugar, firmly packed
1 egg
¼ c. molasses
2¼ c. flour
2 tsp. baking soda
¼ tsp. salt
½ tsp. ground cloves
1 tsp. cinnamon
1 tsp. ginger
⅓ c. granulated sugar

Directions:

1. Preheat oven to 375°.
2. Cream shortening (or shortening and butter); add egg and molasses and beat thoroughly.
3. Combine dry ingredients except for granulated sugar; stir into molasses mixture.
4. Chill dough at least 1 hour.
5. Form dough into 1" diameter balls. Roll each ball in granulated sugar.
6. Place on cookie sheet. Bake 10–12 minutes or until just set. They should be soft. Do not overbake. Makes 4 dozen cookies.

 These cookies will fill your home with the most delicious aroma. They never last long enough to get crisp!

 Since these cookies don't break easily, they travel well in lunch boxes or through the mail.

Pie Crust Cookies

Ingredients:

1 refrigerated pie crust
2 T. butter or margarine, softened
1 tsp. cinnamon
3 tsp. sugar

Directions:

1. Preheat oven to 375°.
2. Spread pie crust with butter or margarine.
3. Sprinkle sugar and cinnamon over dough.
4. Roll up dough and slice into circles.
5. Place on cookie sheet. Bake 8–10 minutes, or until golden. Don't let burn. Makes 1 dozen.

 These cookies were always made with the pie crust scraps when my mother baked pies. Who says you have to bake the pies?! Make a whole batch of cookies from *all* the pie crust! This is the perfect tea party treat.

Raisin Bran Cookies

Ingredients:

2 c. Raisin Bran cereal, crushed to 1½ c.
2 c. flour
1 tsp. baking soda
1 tsp. cinnamon
¾ c. soft margarine or butter
⅔ c. sugar
½ c. brown sugar, packed
2 eggs
1 tsp. vanilla
½ c. raisins (opt.)

Directions:

1. Preheat oven to 325°.
2. Combine cereal, flour, baking soda, and cinnamon.
3. In separate bowl, combine remaining ingredients.
4. Mix two mixtures together; blend well.
5. Drop by teaspoon onto cookie sheets. Bake 15–18 minutes. Makes 3 dozen.

 When cooking with your children, remember to talk to them as you go. They will watch, listen, and learn! Tell them where flour comes from, talk about raisins and how they are made from big, fat grapes. Let them smell and taste the vanilla and cinnamon; use words to describe to them what you are doing as you "combine," "mix," "blend," and "stir." Their vocabularies will grow the more you talk to them!

Ultimate Chocolate Chip Cookies

Ingredients:

1 c. brown sugar, packed
¾ c. sugar
1 c. softened *real* butter
1 tsp. vanilla
2 eggs
2½ c. flour

¾ tsp. salt
¾ tsp. baking soda
1 (12 oz.) pkg. semisweet
   chocolate chips
1 c. chopped walnuts

Directions:

1. Preheat oven to 375°.
2. Beat sugars and butter in large bowl on medium speed until fluffy.
3. Beat in vanilla and eggs.
4. Beat in flour, salt, and baking soda on low speed.
5. Stir in chocolate chips and nuts.
6. Drop dough by the teaspoon onto an ungreased cookie sheet. Flatten slightly with a fork.
7. Bake 8 minutes before removing from cookie sheet. Cool on wire racks. Makes 6 dozen.

 Everyone must have at least one trustworthy recipe for chocolate chip cookies. Take a plate or send a box of these cookies to someone who may be feeling lonely — a college student, an elderly neighbor, or relative. The best way to teach compassion and caring to your children is to let them see you in action, demonstrating it! Talk with them about what it feels like to be lonely and how to make friends.

Festive Cookie Dough

Ingredients:

3½ c. flour
1 tsp. baking powder
1 c. butter
1 (8 oz.) pkg. cream cheese, softened
2 c. sugar
1 egg
1 tsp. vanilla

Directions:

1. Stir together flour and baking powder; set aside.
2. Beat butter and cream cheese on medium for 30 seconds; add sugar; beat until fluffy. Add egg and vanilla; beat well.
3. Gradually add flour mixture to creamed mixture, beating well after each addition.
4. Divide dough into thirds (about 2 cups each). Cover and chill overnight.

Use dough to make the following 3 cookies:

Crackled Crescents

Ingredients:

⅓ festive cookie dough
1 c. miniature semisweet chocolate chips
1 T. shortening

Directions:

1. Preheat oven to 375°.
2. Stir ½ cup chocolate chips into dough.

3. Pinch off small pieces of dough and, with your hands, roll into a crescent shape. Place on ungreased cookie sheet.
4. Bake 8–10 minutes or until edges are firm and bottoms are light golden brown.
5. In small saucepan melt shortening and remaining chocolate over low heat. Dip one end of each cookie into chocolate. Makes 36 cookies.

Little Snow People

Ingredients:

⅓ festive cookie dough
miniature chocolate chips
red cinnamon candies

Directions:

1. Preheat oven to 325°.
2. For each snow person shape dough into 3 balls: one 1" ball, one ¾" ball, and one ½" ball. Place balls on ungreased cookie sheet in decreasing sizes. Press together slightly.
3. Place 2 chocolate pieces into smallest ball for eyes. Press 1 cinnamon candy in middle ball and 2 candies in the largest ball for buttons. Bake 18 minutes; cool 1 minute before removing from cookie sheet. Makes 16 cookies.

Zigzag Cookie Shapes

Ingredients:

⅓ recipe festive cookie dough
1 c. powdered sugar
¼ tsp. vanilla

3–4 tsp. milk
several drops red and
green food coloring

Directions:

1. Preheat oven to 375°.
2. On lightly floured surface roll chilled dough ⅛" thick. Cut out shapes. Place on ungreased cookie sheet.
3. Bake 6–8 minutes. Place on wire rack to cool.
4. To make glaze, stir together powdered sugar, vanilla, and enough milk to make glaze.
5. Divide glaze in half. To one half add red coloring; add green to the other half. Drizzle glaze over cooled cookies in zigzag fashion. Makes about 36 cookies.

 Give your children dough scraps to do with what they please: roll, squeeze, smash, or decorate. Bake in the toaster oven so they can watch them. Dad gets to sample.

Gingerbread People

Ingredients:

½ c. shortening	¾ tsp. salt
½ c. sugar	½ tsp. baking soda
½ c. molasses	¾ tsp. ginger
¼ c. water	¼ tsp. nutmeg
2½ c. flour	⅛ tsp. allspice

Directions:

1. Cream shortening and sugar; add molasses and water.
2. Sift dry ingredients and gradually add to creamed mixture, blending well. Cover; chill 2 or 3 hours.
3. Heat oven to 375°.
4. Roll dough ¼" thick on lightly floured board; cut into desired shapes.
5. Bake on ungreased baking sheet 10–12 minutes. Remove immediately from baking sheet; cool on brown paper or rack. Frost and decorate as desired. Makes about 15 4-inch cookies. Store in tightly closed container.

 Creating gingerbread cookies can become a favorite family tradition. Prepare yourself for an afternoon of fun and mess as you and your helpers create masterpieces. Try decorating cookies to resemble each person in the family. And don't forget pets — everyone looks good in gingerbread!

Honey–Lime Fruit with Frozen Yogurt

Ingredients:

- 2 T. margarine or butter
- 1 T. lime juice
- 1 T. honey
- 2 medium bananas, diagonally-sliced ¼" thick
- ½ c. frozen unsweetened peaches, chopped
- 2 kiwi fruit, peeled and sliced
- 1½ c. halved strawberries
- 2 c. frozen yogurt (strawberry or flavor of your choice)

Directions:

1. In a skillet melt margarine or butter over low heat. Stir in lime juice and honey.
2. Add bananas and peaches. Stir gently 1–2 minutes or until the fruit is heated through.
3. Arrange kiwi fruit and strawberries in dessert bowls; top with frozen yogurt.
4. Spoon warm fruit-honey mixture over all. Serves 7.

 This dessert requires last-minute preparation, but you can have all the ingredients ready to go. Cut the bananas at the last minute to prevent their turning brown. Guests can join you in the kitchen as you put the finishing touches on this dessert.

 Warning: Do not serve honey to a child under one year old. Honey may contain bacterial spores that can cause botulism in young children.

 It is not good to eat too much honey nor is it honorable to seek one's own honor (Proverbs 25:27).

Frozen Fruit Fizz

Ingredients:

2 c. water
2 c. sugar
1 (#2 size) can crushed pineapple, including juice
juice of 3 lemons
1 bottle or can of 7-Up or lemon-lime soda
3 oranges, peeled, sectioned, and cut into small pieces (or 1
    large can mandarin oranges, drained)
3 bananas, sliced
1 package defrosted strawberries, including juice

Directions:

1. Boil water and sugar until sugar is dissolved; cool.
2. Add remainder of ingredients, except 7-Up.
3. Turn into a 3-quart container. Store in freezer.
4. About a half-hour before serving, remove from freezer; spoon into sherbet glasses. Pour about 3 tablespoons 7-Up on each serving.

 This dessert works well after a heavy dinner and equally well as an accompaniment to brunch.

 Freeze this in smaller, individual portions as a "take along" for an ailing friend. Fresh flavors of fruit and soda can brighten up a drab diet. If you time your visit right, the frozen fruit will have turned into the perfect, slushy consistency when you arrive!

Zucchini Dessert Squares

Ingredients:

2 c. flour
¼ tsp. salt
1 c. sugar
½ tsp. cinnamon
¾ c. butter or margarine

Filling:

4–5 c. zucchini, peeled and cubed
⅓ c. lemon juice (juice of 1 lg. lemon)
½ c. sugar
½ tsp. cinnamon
¼ tsp. nutmeg

Directions:

1. Preheat oven to 375°.
2. Combine dry ingredients, then cut in butter.
3. Set aside 3 c. of mixture; pat remaining crumbs into a greased 9" x 13" pan and bake 12 minutes.
4. Meanwhile, heat zucchini and lemon juice until boiling. Reduce heat, cover, and simmer 6–8 minutes.
5. Add sugar, cinnamon, and nutmeg to zucchini mixture; cover and simmer 5 minutes (mixture will be thin). Pour over crust; top with 3 cups crumbs.
6. Bake again for 40–45 minutes. Best served with vanilla ice cream. Makes 16.

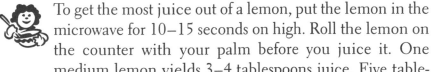 To get the most juice out of a lemon, put the lemon in the microwave for 10–15 seconds on high. Roll the lemon on the counter with your palm before you juice it. One medium lemon yields 3–4 tablespoons juice. Five tablespoons plus one teaspoon equals ⅓ cup juice needed for this recipe.

Peach Cobbler

Ingredients:

½ c. (1 stick) butter
1 qt. sliced peaches or nectarines
¾ c. sugar
½ c. sugar
1 c. milk
1 c. flour
2 tsp. baking powder
½ tsp. salt

Directions:

1. Preheat oven to 350°.
2. Melt butter in 9" x 13" pan.
3. Mix peaches and ¾ cup sugar; spread over butter.
4. In separate bowl, stir remaining ingredients together; pour over peaches. Do not stir.
5. Bake 45 minutes. Serves 12.

 Use frozen, sliced peaches or other fruit when fresh is not available. Peaches don't have to be peeled for this recipe, but if you want to peel them, the easiest way is to drop them into a pot of rapidly boiling water for about 1 minute. Rinse under cold water. The skin will peel off easily.

Apple Tart

Ingredients:

1 c. butter	4 tart, green apples
1 c. sugar	½ c. raisins
1 egg, separated	1 tsp. cinnamon
2 c. flour	½ tsp. water

Directions:

1. Preheat oven to 350°.
2. Cream butter and sugar. Add egg white and stir. Add flour and knead well.
3. Press half of dough mixture into a round springform pan.
4. Peel and slice apples and arrange on dough in pan; sprinkle apples with raisins and cinnamon.
5. Roll out remaining dough. Cut in strips, criss-crossing strips over top.
6. Blend egg yolk with water and brush over crust.
7. Bake one hour. Serve with whipping cream. Serves 10–12.

 A lattice top is easy to do and looks elegant on this tart or any fruit pie. Start with two long strips of dough and place them in cross shape over middle of tart. Add strips, one at a time, working out from center and "weaving" strips as you go, just over and under until you reach the edge.

 As you weave the crust, have your child weave a paper place mat. You'll need colored construction paper, scissors, and tape. First, fold one piece of paper in half; draw cutting lines about 1" apart. Cut along lines, leaving 1" border. Repeat, cutting another sheet into strips of 1". Let child weave his own place mat, alternating the strips of paper.

Pumpkin Bark

Ingredients:

1 c. Bisquick
½ c. brown sugar
½ c. oatmeal
¼ c. butter
1 (16 oz.) can pumpkin
1 (12 oz.) can evaporated
   milk
½ tsp. salt

½ tsp. ginger
2 eggs
¾ c. sugar
1 tsp. cinnamon
¼ tsp. cloves
½ c. nuts
2 T. butter
½ c. brown sugar

Directions:

1. Preheat oven to 350°.
2. Mix Bisquick, brown sugar, oatmeal, and butter until crumbly; press into a 9" x 13" pan. Bake 10 minutes and cool slightly.
3. Mix together all but last 3 ingredients. Pour mixture over crust and bake 20 minutes or until pumpkin has set enough so topping won't sink in.
4. Mix together last 3 ingredients until crumbly. Sprinkle over pumpkin layer and bake 15 minutes longer or until it sets. Serves 18.

 Help your children create a harvest centerpiece. Go for a walk and collect acorns, pods, pine cones, or wildflowers in a basket. When you get home, decorate the table with your finds — and enjoy a square of Pumpkin Bark with apple cider!

Easy Chocolate Microwave Fudge

Ingredients:

2 (16 oz.) pkgs. powdered sugar, sifted
1 c. unsweetened cocoa
½ c. milk
1 c. butter or margarine
1½ c. chopped nuts (opt.)
2 T. vanilla

Directions:

1. In large microwave-safe bowl, mix sugar and cocoa; add milk and butter (do not stir).
2. Heat in microwave on high for 4½–6 minutes, or until butter is melted.
3. Add nuts and vanilla, stirring until smooth.
4. Spread into greased 9" x 13" baking dish. Chill until firm; cut into squares to serve. Serves 24–36.

 For variety add ¾ cup peanut butter instead of nuts. The fudge will have a firmer texture and the flavor will remind you of peanut butter cups.

 Thank someone for their friendship or a service to you! Fudge is a nearly universal language!

Fruit Pizza

Ingredients:

Crust:

½ c. margarine or butter
¾ c. sugar
1 medium egg
1½ c. flour
1 tsp. baking powder
½ tsp. salt
1 tsp. vanilla

Glaze:

½ c. sugar
½ tsp. salt

2 T. cornstarch
½ c. orange juice
2 T. lemon juice
¼ c. water

Filling:

1 (8 oz.) pkg. cream cheese
8 oz. Cool Whip

Topping:

Fruit of your choice

Directions:

1. Start with the crust. Mix margarine, sugar, and egg until light. Stir in vanilla.
2. In another bowl sift together flour, baking powder, and salt.
3. Combine the two mixtures. Shape into a ball, wrap in waxed paper, and refrigerate 1 hour.
4. Meanwhile, make glaze. Cook sugar, salt, cornstarch, orange juice, lemon juice, and water until mixture thickens; remove from heat and let cool.
5. Take crust out of refrigerator and spread on a greased pizza pan; bake at 350° for 10 minutes or until light brown.
6. When crust is cool, make filling. Mix together cream cheese and Cool Whip; spread on crust.
7. Decorate the top with sliced fruit of your choice: grapes, bananas, kiwi, strawberries, etc.
8. Spoon glaze over fruit. (Glaze bananas first to keep from turning dark.) Keep refrigerated. Serves 8–12.

This is easier than it looks ... and it's a great way to serve the delicious fresh fruits of summer. Adapt the fruit choices to the season.

 Let your child help decorate the top of the pizza with fruit.

Apple Crisp

Ingredients:

5–6 c. sliced, tart green apples
1 c. flour
½–1 c. sugar
1 tsp. baking powder
¾ tsp. salt
1 egg, unbeaten
2 T. butter or margarine, melted
½ tsp. cinnamon

Directions:

1. Preheat oven to 350°.
2. Place apples in greased 8" square baking dish.
3. Mix flour, sugar, baking powder, salt, and egg until crumbly; sprinkle over apples.
4. Pour melted butter over topping. Sprinkle with cinnamon.
5. Bake 30–40 minutes until browned nicely. Serve warm, with ice cream. Serves 9.

 Crisp, fresh apples are available in the fall and early winter. Take your children with you to buy the apples. Talk about all the different colors and types of apples.

 Tart, crisp apples that hold their shape are the best apples for baking.

Salted Nut Bars

Ingredients:

3 c. flour
1½ c. brown sugar
1 tsp. salt
1 c. butter or margarine, softened
2 c. mixed nuts, chopped
½ c. corn syrup
2 T. butter
1 T. water
6 oz. butterscotch chips

Directions:

1. Preheat oven to 350°.
2. Combine first 4 ingredients; mix well. Press into 10" x 15" pan and bake 10–12 minutes.
3. Sprinkle nuts over baked crust.
4. Combine last 4 ingredients. Boil 2 minutes, stirring constantly. Pour over nuts.
5. Bake 10–12 minutes. Cool and cut. Makes 3 dozen.

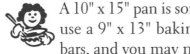 A 10" x 15" pan is sometimes called a "jelly roll pan." If you use a 9" x 13" baking dish, you'll have fewer and thicker bars, and you may need to adjust the baking time.

Chocolate Peanut Butter Bars

Ingredients:

⅓ box (1 pkg.) graham crackers, crushed fine
1 c. (2 sticks) butter, melted
1 c. peanut butter (smooth or crunchy)
2⅔ c. powdered sugar
1 (6 oz.) pkg. milk chocolate chips, or semisweet chips

Directions:

1. Mix crushed graham cracker crumbs, butter, peanut butter, and powdered sugar together. Spread in a thin layer in 9" x 13" pan.
2. Melt chocolate chips and spread over top. Score and refrigerate 2–3 hours. Serves 36.

 Have kids help crush graham crackers. Put the crackers in a zip-closure bag, press the air out of the bag, seal the end, and run a rolling pin back and forth over the crackers.

Blueberry Cake

Ingredients:

1 stick butter, softened	1 ½ c. flour
1 c. sugar	½ c. milk
2 eggs	1 ½ c. fresh blueberries
pinch of salt	1 T. sugar
¾ tsp. baking soda	1 tsp. cinnamon

Directions:

1. Preheat oven to 350°.
2. Cream butter and sugar together; add eggs, one at a time.
3. Add salt, baking soda, flour, and milk
4. Pour into small loaf pan, greased and floured. Drop blueberries over the top. Sprinkle with cinnamon/sugar mixture. Bake 40 minutes. Serves 4–6.

 Don't give in to the temptation to skip the greasing and flouring of the pan; it's the the only way to keep the cake from sticking to it. There is a cooking spray called Baker's Joy which combines flour with the spray.

 Double this recipe so that you have a loaf to take to a friend who has invited you for tea or coffee.

 Share with God's people who are in need. Practice hospitality (Romans 12:13).

Donna's Famous Cake

Ingredients:

1 dark chocolate cake mix
4 T. flour
1 c. milk
1 c. sugar
½ c. shortening
½ c. margarine or butter
2 tsp. vanilla

Directions:

1. Mix and bake cake as directed on box, using two round cake pans.
2. Freeze the cake (don't have to, but cuts easier).
3. Using long, sharp knife, cut each cake horizontally, for a total of 4 layers.
4. Cook flour and milk until thick, stirring often. Let cool.
5. Beat together sugar, shortening, margarine, and vanilla. Add flour mixture, beating until fluffy, approximately 5 minutes.
6. Layer cake and icing, ending with icing on top. Do not frost sides. Keep cool until served. Serves 16 to 20.

 Donna brought this cake to a MOPS spaghetti dinner. But due to uncontrollable circumstances (husbands loitering in the kitchen), it never made it to the serving table.

 Entertaining is so much easier if most of the work is done before the guests arrive. This cake will be an elegant dessert, ready and waiting. Make the cake the day (or even week) before and freeze it until the morning of the party. Assemble cake as it thaws. It will stay cool and be perfect for guests.

Earthquake Cake

Ingredients:

1–2 c. coconut
1 c. chopped nuts
1 German chocolate cake mix
½ c. margarine or butter
1 (8 oz.) pkg. cream cheese
1 lb. powdered sugar
pinch of salt

Directions:

1. Preheat oven to 350°.
2. Grease a 10" x 15" jelly roll pan.
3. Cover bottom with as much coconut as you like. Sprinkle chopped nuts over coconut.
4. Mix cake mix as directed. Pour over coconut and nuts.
5. Combine margarine and cream cheese. Mix in powdered sugar and salt until creamy and fluffy.
6. Dollop over unbaked cake; do not stir.
7. Bake 25 minutes or until done. Serves 18.

This cake splits across the top, giving it its name. Have the kids help spread the coconut and nuts in the pan.

 A misprinted recipe for Chocolate Zucchini Cake called for too much baking soda, vinegar, and flour. The whole thing erupted like a volcano in my oven, oozing into cracks and crevices, never to be seen again. A year later my kitchen still smelled like charbroiled Chocolate Zucchini Cake every time I turned on the oven.

Graham Cracker Eclair Cake

Ingredients:

2 small boxes instant vanilla pudding
2 c. milk
12 oz. Cool Whip
1 (1 lb.) box graham crackers
1 can chocolate frosting

Directions:

1. Blend pudding with milk; fold in Cool Whip.
2. Place a layer of crackers in 9" x 13" pan; top with half the pudding mixture.
3. Top with another layer of crackers, followed by remaining pudding mixture.
4. Top with another layer of crackers.
5. Melt frosting in microwave for about 1 minute and pour over top layer.
6. Refrigerate overnight. Serves 16–20.

 One mom's comfort food: Graham crackers and cocoa. "During a long and difficult pregnancy these were among the few foods I could keep down. They still remind me of those cozy days of waiting on the couch."

 This easy, no-bake recipe can be made the night before when you need something to take to a meeting.

Pumpkin Cake

Ingredients:

1 yellow cake mix
  (reserve 1 c. of mix)
1 stick (½ c.) butter, melted
1 egg

2 heaping tsp. pumpkin
  pie spice
¼ tsp. nutmeg
¼ tsp. ginger

Filling:
1 (29 oz.) can of pumpkin
2 eggs
¾ c. sugar
⅔ c. milk
¼ tsp. salt

Topping:
1 c. cake mix
½ stick butter, softened
¼ c. sugar
1 tsp. cinnamon

Directions:

1. Preheat oven to 350°.
2. Treat 9" x 13" baking dish with nonstick spray.
3. Mix first 3 ingredients well and press into pan.
4. Mix filling ingredients and pour over bottom layer.
5. Mix topping ingredients until crumbly; sprinkle over pumpkin.
6. Bake 45 minutes or until done in center. Serves 18.

 The lower-fat margarines (often packaged in a tub rather than a stick) are not necessarily appropriate for baking. Check the label. For baking cookies or cakes, use a product that contains no less than 60 percent vegetable oil.

Oatmeal Cake

Ingredients:

½ c. oatmeal, quick or
   regular
2¼ c. water
1½ c. sugar
1½ c. brown sugar
¾ c. butter, softened
3 eggs
1½ tsp. cinnamon
¾ tsp. salt
2¼ c. flour
1½ tsp. soda

Topping:
½ c. butter, melted
1 c. nuts
1 c. coconut
½ c. brown sugar
¼ c. milk
1 tsp. vanilla

Directions:

1. Preheat oven to 350°.
2. Bring water to a boil; add oatmeal to water and let stand 10 minutes.
3. Combine rest of cake ingredients; add oat mixture, mixing well.
4. Treat 9" x 13" pan with nonstick spray. Pour mixture into pan and bake 40 minutes.
5. While cake is baking mix topping ingredients. Spread on warm cake; broil until bubbly. Serves 18.

 When your rubber spatula gets battered edges, just trim them off. Your spatula will be good for many more baking sessions. After several trimmings it can still be used to scrape the contents out of narrow-necked bottles.

Lemon Cake

Ingredients:

1 white cake mix
¾ c. vegetable oil
4 eggs
1 (3 oz.) pkg. lemon jello
1 c. hot water
1 tsp. vanilla

Glaze:

1 c. powdered sugar
3 T. lemon juice

Directions:

1. Prehcat oven to 350°.
2. Add oil and eggs to cake mix.
3. Dissolve jello in hot water and combine with mix; stir in vanilla.
4. Pour batter into 9" x 13" pan. Bake 30 minutes.
5. Remove from oven and immediately pour glaze over top. Serves 12.

 If you use a fresh lemon for the glaze, after you've squeezed the juice out of the lemon slice the shell into smaller pieces and drop them into your sink's garbage disposer. Run hot water as you run the disposer — you'll freshen the sink quickly with a nice citrus aroma.

 I had just finished making a bundt cake for my son's Cub Scout cake auction and was about to drizzle frosting on top when I was called away from the kitchen. Taking advantage of my absence, our 100-pound dog decided to take a huge bite out of the cake. As I wondered what to do, my son suggested cutting away the part the dog ate, leaving the letter "C" for Cub Scouts. My cake brought the highest bid that night, and I received many compliments on my creativity!

Zebra Cake

Ingredients:

1 chocolate cake mix with pudding in it
1 (8 oz.) cream cheese, softened
1 egg
⅓ c. sugar
1 (8 oz.) container Cool Whip
1 (16 oz.) can Hershey's syrup

Directions:

1. Prepare cake mix as directed.
2. Before baking, mix together cream cheese, egg, and sugar. Spoon this mixture randomly over the cake batter in the pan and swirl it through batter with a knife.
3. Bake according to package directions. Cool cake completely.
4. Mix desired amount of chocolate syrup into Cool Whip. Spread chocolate Cool Whip over cake. Drizzle more syrup randomly over the top.
5. Store cake in refrigerator. Serves 18.

 I made a castle birthday cake for my son, complete with Hershey bar drawbridges. Unfortunately, an hour into the party the cake collapsed from its weight and became a haunted house.

 The lions may grow weak and hungry, but those who seek the LORD lack no good thing (Psalm 34:10).

Chocolate Chip Brownie Torte

Ingredients:

¾ c. cocoa
½ tsp. baking soda
⅔ c. margarine or butter, melted and divided
½ c. boiling water
2 c. sugar
2 eggs, slightly beaten
1⅓ c. flour
1 tsp. vanilla
6 oz. semisweet miniature chocolate bits

Cream Frosting:

2 c. heavy cream (or whipped topping), chilled
¼ c. powdered sugar
1 tsp. vanilla
6 oz. semisweet miniature chocolate bits

Directions:

1. Preheat oven to 350°.
2. Chill bowl and beaters for frosting.
3. Line 9" x 13" pan with waxed paper or parchment paper and grease it.
4. Combine cocoa and baking soda; stir in ⅓ cup melted butter. Bring water to a boil and add to mixture, stirring until thick.
5. Stir in sugar, eggs, and remaining butter until smooth.
6. Add flour and vanilla, stirring to blend completely. Stir in 1 cup miniature chocolate bits.
7. Bake 20 minutes or until brownies begin to pull away from sides of pan. Cool 10 minutes.
8. Sprinkle top of brownies with powdered sugar to prevent sticking. Invert onto smooth cutting board (or counter). Remove foil. Refrigerate 30 minutes.

9. While brownies are cooling, beat all frosting ingredients except chocolate bits until stiff (about 2 minutes).
10. Cut brownie the short way into 4 equal pieces. Place each piece on cake plate.
11. Spread about ¾ cup frosting (about ¼" thick) over sides and top of each piece.
12. Throw bits of chocolate on top and sides of each piece.
13. Chill at least 1 hour. Keep refrigerated. Cut into 20 slices. Serves 20.

 Chilling a mixing bowl and beaters will increase the volume of the whipped cream.

 This is an elegant dessert that serves a crowd and can be made ahead. One less thing to worry about on the big night.

Cookie Dough Brownies

Ingredients:

2 c. sugar
1½ c. flour
½ c. baking cocoa
½ tsp. salt
1 c. vegetable oil
2 eggs
2 tsp. vanilla
½ c. chopped walnuts or
    pecans (opt.)

Filling:

½ c. butter or margarine,
    softened
½ c. brown sugar, packed

¼ c. sugar
2 T. milk
1 tsp. vanilla
1 c. flour

Glaze:

1 c. (6 oz.) semisweet
    chocolate chips
1 T. shortening
¾ c. chopped walnuts or
    pecans

Directions:

1. Preheat oven to 350°.
2. Combine sugar, flour, cocoa and salt. Add oil, eggs, and vanilla. Beat at medium speed for 3 minutes.
3. Stir in nuts, if desired. Pour into a greased 13" x 9" x 2" baking pan.
4. Bake 30 minutes or until brownies test done. Cool completely.
5. For filling, cream butter and sugars; add milk and vanilla; mix well. Beat in flour and spread over brownies. Chill until firm.
6. Melt chocolate chips and shortening in saucepan, stirring until smooth. Spread over filling. Immediately sprinkle with nuts, pressing down slightly. Makes 3 dozen.

 This recipe makes so many brownies you will be able to share the wealth. Take a dozen on a pretty paper plate to a new neighbor on your block.

Sinful Brownies

Ingredients:

1 (14 oz.) package caramels (49 caramels)
¾ c. butter, melted
1 German chocolate cake mix
⅔ c. canned evaporated milk, divided
1 (12 oz.) pkg. chocolate chips
1 c. chopped nuts, divided

Directions:

1. Preheat oven to 350°.
2. In double boiler or microwave melt caramels in ⅓ cup evaporated milk.
3. Melt butter and add to dry cake mix with remaining ⅓ cup evaporated milk.
4. Grease and flour 9" x 13" baking dish. Press half of cake mixture lightly into pan; bake 10–15 minutes.
5. Remove from oven; sprinkle with chocolate chips.
6. Pour caramels over chocolate chips; sprinkle nuts over caramels.
7. Spoon in remaining cake mix and dot remaining nuts by teaspoon over top. Bake again for 15–20 minutes. Cool. Cut into squares. Makes 24–30.

 Your children can help unwrap the caramels (but you'd better buy an extra bag to be sure enough make it into the bowl as well as into their mouths)!

Disappearing Marshmallow Brownies

Ingredients:

1 c. butterscotch morsels
½ c. margarine or butter
1½ c. flour
⅔ c. brown sugar, packed
2 tsp. baking powder
½ tsp. salt
1 tsp. vanilla
2 eggs
2 c. mini marshmallows
2 c. semisweet chocolate morsels

Directions:

1. Preheat oven to 350°.
2. Melt butterscotch morsels and margarine in a large bowl in the microwave. Stir. Cool to lukewarm.
3. Add flour, brown sugar, baking powder, salt, vanilla, and eggs to butterscotch mixture; mix well.
4. Fold in marshmallows and chocolate morsels.
5. Spread in a lightly greased 9" x 13" pan. Bake 25 minutes. Do not overbake. Center will still be jiggly but becomes firm when cool. Makes 16–24.

 Stock a bottom kitchen drawer with measuring cups, wooden spoons, plastic bowls, and cookie cutters so he can play cooking while you bake. Change items periodically.

 When freezing brownies or bar cookies, freeze before cutting them. They will retain moisture and not dry out when you thaw them.

Carrot Bars

Ingredients:

2 c. granulated sugar
2 c. flour
½ tsp. salt
3 tsp. baking powder
3 tsp. cinnamon
4 eggs
1¼ c. salad oil
3 cups carrots, grated
1 cup nuts, chopped

Frosting:
½ c. butter
1 (8 oz.) pkg. cream cheese
1 lb. powdered sugar
1 tsp. vanilla

Directions:

1. Preheat oven to 350°.
2. Mix dry ingredients in small bowl.
3. Mix remaining ingredients except nuts; combine with first mixture and mix well.
4. Blend in nuts. Bake in greased 12" x 15" jelly roll pan about 20–30 minutes; remove from oven and cool.
5. Cream butter and cream cheese; add powdered sugar and vanilla. Beat until light and fluffy.
6. Frost cake after it is cool. Serves 24.

 Keep snack-sized candy bars in the freezer to have on hand for special treats. Surprise overnight guests by placing a candy on their pillows.

Key Lime Pie

Ingredients:

1 small container Cool Whip (2½–3 c.)
1 (14 oz.) can Eagle Brand sweetened condensed milk
green food coloring (opt.)
¼–⅓ c. key lime juice
1 prepared graham cracker crust

Directions:

1. Mix Cool Whip, condensed milk, food color, and lime juice until well blended.
2. Pour into crust and freeze until firm. Garnish with lime slices, if desired. Serves 8.

 Key lime juice is worth looking for — ask the grocery store manager to order it if you can't find it.

 Serve Key Lime Pie at a backyard barbecue. It goes well with Mexican, tropical, or barbecue menus.

Kentucky Chocolate Chip Pie

Ingredients:

3 eggs
¾ c. brown sugar
⅔ c. light corn syrup
¼ c. butter, melted
½ c. oatmeal, *un*cooked
1 tsp. vanilla
½ c. chocolate chips
8" refrigerated pie crust

Directions:

1. Preheat oven to 350°.
2. Beat eggs until foamy. Add sugar; beat well.
3. Add corn syrup and butter to egg mixture; mix well.
4. Stir in oats, vanilla, and chocolate chips.
5. Pour into unbaked pie shell. Bake 45 minutes, until firm in center. Enjoy warm or cold. Serves 8.

 Remember parsley and whipping cream! Almost any culinary catastrophe can be salvaged with the wise placement of one or the other.

 Above all, love each other deeply, because love covers over a multitude of sins. Offer hospitality to one another without grumbling (1 Peter 4:8–9).

Hello Dolly Pie

Ingredients:

1 stick butter, melted
1½ c. crushed graham crackers (about 1 pkg.)
1 (14 oz.) can sweetened condensed milk
1 c. chocolate chips
1 c. coconut
1 c. chopped walnuts or pecans

Directions:

1. Preheat oven to 350°.
2. Melt butter in glass pie pan in oven or microwave. Add graham cracker crumbs, pressing together with butter to make crust.
3. Pour condensed milk directly onto the crust.
4. Layer with chips, coconut, and nuts. Press down onto the shell.
5. Bake 30–35 minutes. Serves 8.

 Your guests will savor Hello Dolly Pie whether you've served them dinner or they've just come for dessert. Eat by candlelight — the aura makes people want to linger and talk.

Lemon Bread Pudding

Ingredients:

6–8 slices of bread (day-old white, French, rolls—whatever
   you have on hand)
4 c. milk
½ c. sugar
4 eggs
1½ tsp. lemon extract

Directions:

1. Preheat oven to 350°.
2. Tear bread into pieces and place in 9" x 13" baking dish (crust
   may be left on or trimmed off, as desired).
3. Beat remaining ingredients together and pour over bread pieces.
4. Bake 30–40 minutes or until custard is firm. Do not overbake.
   Serve warm or cold. May be served with ice cream or Cool
   Whip for dessert. Recipe may be halved, using 8" x 8" baking
   dish. Serves 12.

 One mom's comfort food: "My grandmother made lemon
bread pudding for me when I was a baby. I grew up with it
and I've used it as baby food for my own five children."

 My four-year-old son was a cake fanatic and perked up
when he heard we were having angel food cake for dessert.
I could see the wheels turning in his head about the name
of this dessert he had never had before. As I placed a fluffy
wedge in front of him, he looked up innocently and whis-
pered, "Mommy, is this one of the wings?"

Orange Tapioca Pudding

Ingredients:

3 c. water
2 (3 oz.) pkg. tapioca pudding
1 (3 oz.) pkg. orange jello
1 (8 oz.) carton Cool Whip
2 (11 oz.) cans mandarin oranges, drained

Directions:

1. Boil water; add to puddings and jello. Boil mixture over medium low heat 10 minutes, stirring frequently; cool.
2. Add Cool Whip and oranges.
3. Chill until firm. Serves 12.

 A light dessert. Peaches and peach jello could be substituted for oranges and orange jello.

 Is it time to clean the coffeemaker? If your coffee is tasting bitter and you don't think it's your brand of coffee, "brew" a mixture of white vinegar and water. Pour the hot vinegar/water solution back into the coffeemaker and let it sit 30 minutes. "Brew" it again and discard. Finally, brew once with clean water.

Butterscotch Ice Cream Delight

Ingredients:

½ c. brown sugar
2 sticks (1 c.) butter or margarine, melted
½ c. oatmeal
1 c. chopped pecans, chopped
2 c. flour
2 jars Kraft caramel syrup
½ gallon French vanilla ice cream

Directions:

1. Preheat oven to 400°.
2. Mix all ingredients except caramel syrup and ice cream.
3. Spread on cookie sheet; bake 15 minutes.
4. Crumble while hot. Spread half the crumbs over bottom of 9" x 13" glass pan.
5. Set one jar caramel syrup in warm water to soften; drizzle over crumbs.
6. Soften and spread ice cream over mixture.
7. Set second jar caramel syrup in warm water to soften; spread over all.
8. Top with remaining crumbs. Freeze and cut as needed. Serves 20.

 Keep this dessert in the freezer for a busy day. Line the pan with foil before assembling. After the dessert has frozen solid, pop it out of the dish, wrap it securely, and store it in the freezer so you don't give up the use of your pan. When you're ready to serve, unwrap the foil, place the frozen dessert in the 9" x 13" pan, and serve.

Pink Lemonade Ice Cream Pie

Ingredients:

¾ c. gingersnaps
⅔ c. graham cracker crumbs
1 T. sugar
¼ c. butter or margarine, melted
1 qt. vanilla ice cream, softened
1 (6 oz.) can frozen pink lemonade concentrate, thawed

Directions:

1. Preheat oven to 350°.
2. Crush gingersnaps. Mix crumbs, sugar, and butter.
3. Treat 9" pie pan with nonstick spray. Press mixture firmly and evenly over bottom and sides of pan. Bake 10 minutes; cool.
4. Combine ice cream and lemonade in bowl; mix well. Pour into crust.
5. Freeze until firm.
6. Garnish with fresh peach slices, if desired. Serves 6–8.

 If you don't have gingersnaps, you can use all graham crackers for the crust, or use a prepared graham cracker crust.

 One mom's comfort food: "I like to sit in the bathtub with a cub of Jasmine Tea and a bowl of Rocky Road Ice Cream or Peach Sorbet with a banana in it."

Ice Cream Cake

Ingredients:

First Layer:

24 Oreo cookies, crushed
¼ c. butter, melted

Second Layer:

½ gallon any flavor ice cream, softened

Third Layer:

1 (16 oz.) can chocolate syrup
1 (14 oz.) can sweetened condensed milk
½ c. butter
1 tsp. vanilla

Fourth Layer:

8 oz. Cool Whip

Directions:

1. Combine Oreos and melted butter and press into 9" x 13" pan. Freeze ½ hour. (Take ice cream out to soften when you put the Oreos into the freezer.)
2. Spread softened ice cream over top of oreo layer and freeze ½ hour.
3. Bring chocolate syrup, condensed milk, and butter to a boil, stirring continually for 3–5 minutes; add vanilla and cool. Spread over ice cream; freeze ½ hour.
4. Top with Cool Whip and garnish with cookie crumbs. Freeze 24 hours. Serves 20.

 This recipe can use any flavor of ice cream. Imagine the possibilities — peppermint, butter pecan, coffee fudge, chocolate chip. This could be someone's ultimate "comfort" food.

Pineapple–Buttermilk Sherbet

Ingredients:

1 qt. buttermilk
1¼–1½ c. sugar
1 (10 oz.) can crushed pineapple with juice
1 rounded c. frozen or fresh strawberries (or frozen or
    fresh blueberries)
2 tsp. vanilla

Directions:

1. Mix together all ingredients. Ladle into 9" x 13" pan lined with
   waxed paper.
2. Freeze and cut into squares. Serves 16.
3. Optional: May also be frozen in popsicle molds. Try this light,
   low-fat treat for a summer refresher.

 Talk about buttermilk, whole milk, skim milk, and cream.
Let your child taste the different types and help her find
good words to describe the differences.

 Don't apologize for how your house looks, drawing attention to the problems. Instead, welcome your guests with
joy. Remember, they came to see you!

APPENDIXES

❨ Picky Eaters ❩

Mealtimes with young children require lots of understanding, patience, and flexibility. It is very possible that your young child is not hungry when you plunk the plates on the table. Maybe he has liked green beans for months, but you are pestering him to hurry and eat them tonight, and he would rather exert his autonomy than eat the green beans. Maybe she is more interested in the playhouse she was making with a friend when you called her to dinner than about anything on her plate. What can you do on nights like these?

Here are some strategies that may help:

- Serve small portions to your child. A toddler requires about half the size portion of an adult. Don't overwhelm him with a mound of food.
- Let your child help you prepare the meal. If he has torn the lettuce and tossed the ingredients, he will be more likely to taste the salad.
- Think of a few clever, positive things to say — the kind of things your children will quote you for when they're adults, such as "Your eyes say they don't like it, but your mouth might say otherwise," or "Don't worry, you're just not old enough yet to like spaghetti. But try a bite, because you never know when the day may come."

- Experiment with new recipes and foods. Talk about the star fruit you found at the supermarket. Try preparing spaghetti squash. Not only will you be modeling an adventuresome spirit about food, you will surely find some things he likes. And meal preparation will be more fun for you, too!
- If your child doesn't like anything on his plate, allow him to get or prepare something of his own (yogurt, banana, peanut butter sandwich) and return to the table with it. This should help avoid your becoming a short order cook.
- Let your child sit and not eat if she chooses. But if she proceeds to play with the food, it's time to remove her plate.
- Snacking, or eating several small meals, can be nutritious for a child if she's eating a variety of healthful foods. But if she's snacking just before dinner, you have sabotaged the meal. Often toddlers fill up on milk or juice and are not hungry for meals. Encourage her to eat first, then nurse or take a cup or bottle.
- Limit distractions at the table, particularly the TV. If dinner is a three-ring circus, why should a child care about the food?
- Be clear and consistent about the behavior you expect at the table. Your child doesn't need to throw food, or climb on the table, or sit in your lap so that you are unable to eat. You may want to excuse your young children after they have finished, so that you and your spouse can linger together over a cup of coffee.
- Be willing to forego food battles. You can't make your child eat; if you could, you couldn't make him like it. If you engage in this battle, you're in danger of the struggle itself becoming more significant than the food. Eating together should be low-stress and fun. If your child has Mom and Dad's attention — with lots of laughter and conversation — at the table, that is where he will want to be. One day it will strike you that your picky eater is not so picky anymore.

❨The Road to Hospitality❩

Any mom can entertain guests in her home. Hospitality is not a magical, mystical gift that has been bequeathed to some, leaving the rest of us destined to be guests 'til the end of time. Hospitality is about giving. It provides you and your family with the opportunity to share yourselves, time, food, and fun; it should never be about perfection, obligation, or dread.

When thinking of entertaining, consider the following:

- *What do you want to teach your children through the exercise of hospitality?* Compassion, graciousness, kindness, love? This prayer is one family's "north star" for hospitality. It reminds them of what really matters to their family.

Prayer of Welcome

O God, make the door of this house wide enough to receive all who need human love and fellowship, narrow enough to shut out all envy, pride and strife. Make its threshold smooth enough to be no stumbling block, but rugged and strong enough to turn back the tempter's power. God, make the door of this house the gateway to Thine eternal Kingdom, through Jesus Christ, our Lord, Amen.

— seen inside the doorway of
The Old Rectory at Crowhhurst, Sussex, England

- *What is your idea of hospitality?* What do you value most? Be honest with yourself. Are you an extrovert who loves company and activity? Then you'll enjoy larger gatherings more than the introvert, who will be more comfortable with a few people at a time in a quieter setting.

- *What is your and your family's style?* Most families with young children automatically think casual. But think about what you really enjoy doing. Are impromptu, spur-of-the-moment get-togethers with friends your favorites, or do you enjoy pulling together a more formal dinner, like Thanksgiving or Christmas? Or are you most happy when your guests are in the kitchen, with everyone pitching in with the cooking and serving?

- *Set reasonable expectations.* If your kitchen is small, or your tolerance for high levels of activity is low, consider entertaining with teas, coffees, or dessert parties, where most of the preparation can be done in advance and you can be free to visit with your guests. The truth is, you will find that your ability to entertain and your desires will fluctuate. How much sleep your little ones allow you to get in a night, how many children you have under the age of five, and your physical condition will all influence your decisions.

- *Explore different dishes and cuisines.* As you entertain, you will discover some dishes that suit you very well. Make these your specialties. You don't have to prepare something new or exotic every time you entertain. Having a few menus you know you can prepare easily will set you free to invite the new neighbors over for dinner without panicking.

- *Develop rituals and traditions.* As you develop specialties and your own style, you will be establishing traditions that will build your family and strengthen friendships. Traditions aren't just things we do, but also how we do things. The time spent in preparation will be equally as important as the end result; for example, having your children help make a special candy every Christmas. And don't forget to include ethnic dishes from your family backgrounds as you create traditions.

- *Involve your family.* Enlist the help of your husband, friends, children, baby-sitters, whoever is available. Let your family know what your plans are and how you need their help and understanding.
- *Decide on a serving option.* There are four basic serving options when entertaining. Choose the one that best fits your home, style, menu, and guests.
  1. The buffet: Set up the food in an attractive arrangement and let the guests serve themselves. This is a good choice for large groups and/or open kitchens. In a smaller space, you can set up several "stations," with salad in one room, the entrée in another.
  2. The prepared plate: This involves dishing up the food in the kitchen and serving each guest at the table. This method allows for portion control and attractive presentation, and eliminates having to look at dirty serving dishes. It works best if you have a helper to bring the plates to the table for you.
  3. Family-style: Bring the bowls and platters to the table and let the guests pass the food.
  4. Pass the platter: If your table isn't large enough to hold the platters for family-style, you or a helper can hand the platters to the guests and allow them to serve themselves. This keeps the table clear.
- *Other dining considerations:*
  — Are there any allergies or diet concerns you need to take into account? This doesn't mean you need to cook several different menus for guests, but you may be able to plan one selection that can be adapted to take care of special needs.
  — Pick your main course and plan the rest of the menu around it.
  — Select serving pieces and utensils. If they need cleaning or polishing, do it early.

— Plan recipes that can be prepared in stages. Many dishes can be prepared ahead and kept in the freezer or refrigerator until the day of the event. If you are the solo cook, don't plan more than one recipe that will need last-minute attention.

— Be sure all the food will fit in the freezer, refrigerator, or oven when it needs to. If your refrigerator is crammed with appetizers and salads, be sure to have a dessert that comes from the oven, or that can wait at room temperature.

— Check the temperatures and times for oven preparations. If you are cooking with only one oven, it is efficient to plan on two things cooking together (potatoes and roast, for example). But if one dish cooks at 425° for 1 hour and one at 325° for 30 minutes, you'll have to make other choices.

— Choose a main dish that does not involve critical timing.

— Choose side dishes that balance and don't overwhelm the flavors of the main dish. Also, think about the color on the plate. Try to avoid serving an entirely beige meal (chicken, potatoes, bread, custard, etc.). Splashes of color stimulate the eye and the appetite.

— Avoid side dishes that don't hold well, in case dinner is running late. If you're serving pasta, select something like ravioli, which can be cooked ahead and reheated, rather than noodles, which can be easily overcooked into a mushy clump.

— Looking for a salad? Don't forget the always popular Caesar. It is easy to prepare and goes with almost every kind of meal.

— Match the dessert to the dinner. A heavy meal of meat and potatoes can be finished with a lighter dessert of fruit, meringues, mousse, or custards. A lighter meal of soup, fish, or chicken can handle a richer, heavier dessert.

— You don't have to prepare everything from scratch or by yourself. Purchase the rolls, buy dessert or serve ice cream, or ask guests each to bring an item.

- *Add an element of fun to your entertaining:*
  - Have music in the background to add to the atmosphere. You can even use a theme. If you're serving barbecue, play country music. Italian dinner, try opera. A tropical feast? Check out Hawaiian music from the library.
  - Use place cards to create interesting conversations at the table. This is a great job for children. Miniature pumpkins or gourds with the names written on them work well for a fall meal. For an Italian dinner, spell the names out using pasta. For Easter, write with markers on dyed eggs.
  - Decorate the table. Table decorations can carry through a theme for the party. Use simple things from your home. Try apples with candles inserted at center, or a random collection of candles in different holders.
  - Have a bingo game, or other simple table game for the children to play while sitting at the table. Small prizes (candy bars, a quarter, a box of crayons) can be wrapped and tucked into the table decorations. Be sure to arrange it so every child wins something.
  - Have someone take Polaroid pictures of the guests and cooks as the dinner is being prepared. (Try this one at a picnic or barbecue). The pictures can be a take-home souvenir of the evening.
- *Expect glitches.* Tempers flare, patience snaps, roasts burn. It happens. Things don't have to be perfect to be successful. Don't panic. When a problem arises — and it will — step back, take a breath, and look for a solution. Above all, never, never criticize aspects of your own party. If you don't mention it, most people won't pay any attention to shortcomings. But if you talk about the vegetable being overcooked, people will notice. Be kind to yourself!
- Arrive in style. Plan your preparation time to allow yourself thirty minutes or so before the party just to relax. Some options: (1) invite a good friend to come a little early to give you the break; (2) hire a baby-sitter to come in for an hour; or

(3) have your spouse watch the children and help with a few details. If you are relaxed and have fun, your guests will have fun too. Don't put unnecessary pressure on yourself. Decide what you can do, do the best you can, and enjoy the results.

❰Evey Talks Turkey❱

A few years ago the slang expression for someone who was a bonehead, a klutz, generally annoying, or incompetent, was "You turkey!" Now we know where the expression comes from. When we asked moms to send us their greatest kitchen catastrophes, a large percentage of them revolved around the preparation of that most-American feast that we want to be so perfect: Thanksgiving dinner.

If it's your turn to cook Thanksgiving dinner this year, if the Grannies and Grandpas and cousins and in-laws are coming to your house, here are some tips from two older birds: At least a week before Thanksgiving, sit down at the kitchen table with paper, a pencil, your recipe card box, and a cup of hot tea. It's time to plan Thanksgiving dinner.

- *Make a menu.* Are there any food allergies or strong likes or dislikes you must contend with? Choose the recipes you want to prepare. Browse through magazines if you want, or call your mother or a friend who has a great recipe you'd like to try. Just remember not to experiment on more than one or two new recipes, so you feel confident preparing most of the meal.
- *Get help!* Guests are usually more than happy to know how they can help you with the meal. Ask someone to bring rolls,

someone to bring stuffing, someone to bring the pumpkin pies. Your guests will feel they've been able to contribute and can enjoy your company more because you won't be so wiped out. Remember, Thanksgiving is for pilgrims, not martyrs!

- *Prepare a grocery list.* If you are serving turkey, determine the size you need by the number of people you're serving. For a bird of 12 pounds or less, allow one pound per adult. For birds that weigh more than 12 pounds, count on ¾ pound for each serving. If you want to buy only a turkey breast (for a smaller gathering), figure ½ pound per person. Buy either a turkey with one of those no-fool, pop-up-when-it's-done red buttons, or else buy a meat thermometer. You don't want to guess on when the turkey is done.

- *Table decoration.* Add to your shopping list such things as candles, silver polish, a centerpiece, and place cards. Place cards are a bit of old-fashioned etiquette that serve some wonderful real-life purposes. With place cards you can predetermine who will sit next to whom at the table. Let's face it, sometimes there are people who would love to sit together, and people who really wouldn't!

  If you want to spark some conversation at the table, on the underside of each place card write a question that person will have to answer during the meal. Write questions that have no right or wrong answer, but will provide some insight into the respondent. At this particular holiday, use a theme of thanksgiving.

  What is one thing you are thankful your parents didn't give you?

  Tell about one experience you came through thankful just to be alive.

  What is one quality you appreciate about the person on your right?

  What blessing are you particularly thankful for today?

- *Thawing and cooking the turkey.* Start with the time at which you would like to serve dinner and work backward, planning on paper the steps you'll take to reach your goal of having everything ready at the same time. Study your frozen turkey. Read the instructions on the packaging for thawing and cooking. You want to get the bird thawed, but not have it thawed too long before you cook it.

Keep the turkey in the freezer until it is time to thaw it. Figure that thawing will take one day in the refrigerator for every five pounds of bird. The night before you want to cook it, press on the meat with your finger. If it doesn't "give," it's still frozen. If it is frozen, put it in the sink — still in its original packaging — and cover with cold water. Change the water every few hours. Do not thaw at room temperature or in warm water.

When you unwrap the bird, remove the extraneous parts from bags in both the upper and lower cavities of the turkey. First pull open the flap of skin at the top of the bird, and pull out the neck. Pry open the legs at the bottom and pull out bags of giblets. You can prepare these or toss them out, as you prefer — but the main thing is to get them out of the bird! Rinse the bird and pat dry with paper towels.

Many magazines carry "how to cook the perfect turkey" articles in their November issues, so look for one of them or find a recipe in a trusted cookbook. If you cook stuffing in the bird, don't stuff it until you are ready to put it into the oven.

Cook the turkey in a roasting pan. Disposable roasting pans are sold in supermarkets around the holidays, but a large covered roaster is fairly inexpensive and may be a good investment for years to come.

- *Prepare ahead.* Prepare as much of the meal as possible the day before: the dessert, rolls, perhaps a potato casserole or a molded cranberry salad. And set the table the day before so you can see if you've forgotten anything, and also so that you and your family can enjoy the lovely table and the anticipation of an excellent meal with family or friends.
- *Carving the turkey.* Think through who should have the honor of carving the turkey — preferably someone who

knows how, or who would enjoy learning. Consult a basic cookbook for a diagram on how to carve a turkey. Salvage the wishbone and dry it on the window ledge until the time seems right to have a wishbone pulling contest.

- *Cleaning up.* After the feast, when you're too stuffed to move and every glass, plate, and serving dish you own is dirty, either delegate chores or at the least accept help that is offered you. Then you, too, can watch the football game, or play in a backyard football game, or take a long leisurely autumn walk. And if you are still stuck in the kitchen, at least you'll have someone to keep you company.

(Contributors)

*E*ach of these women contributed recipes, catastrophes, or comfort foods, or they tested recipes. We are grateful to every one! If we have missed or misspelled your name, please accept our apologies, and let us know.

Allen, Nancy
Allen, Ashley
Anderson, Linda
Anway, Debbie
Aprahamian, Valerie
Bachara, Jackie
Bailey, Alicia
Baldeck, Lisa
Baldwin, Jean
Banks, Ailene
Barbaro, Shari
Barlow, Bonnie
Barnes, Lisa
Barnett, Lori
Bartlett, Conny
Basore, Marcie
Baylor, Judith
Bennett, Shannon
Berensky, Wendy
Bettinger, Susan
Bettis, Jean
Betts, Marigene
Betzner, April

Bienz, Susan
Bilquist, Julie
Birkestrand, Sherry
Bittle, Cindy
Bixler, Deanna
Bjork, Cha-Cha
Black, Cari
Boersma, Betty
Bolton, Jean
Boot, Janice
Bostic, Linda
Botley, Dawn
Bove, Jennifer
Bowes, Susan
Bowman, Brenda
Brauer, Julie
Brenner, Angela
Brown, Paula
Browning, Tia
Browolert, Melanie
Bruick, Jan
Brunettka, D.
Brunick, Jan

Bulaich, Cindy
Burge, Barb
Burnett, Teresa
Burns Holly
Burton, Laurie
Buyers, Laurie
Byacich, Cindy
Cabalan, J.
Cadicamo, Denise
Cahalan, Patty
Callison, Dawn
Cardamone, Kim
Careswell, Lori
Carrico, Susan
Carroll, Brandi
Carter, Belinda
Casale, Barbara Ann
Cassell, Joyce
Cecere, Maryann
Cerceo, Susan
Chambers, Karen
Clark, Crystal
Clark, Criplie

Cliff, Diane
Connor, Debbie
Cox, Nancy
Cox, Cheri
Craker, Liz
Crawford, Cindy
Creekmur, Stacy
Crocker, Nancy
Crockett, Lori
Cuchiara, Debbie
Cultice, Kris
Cummins, Cheryl
Curtis, Hope
Curtis, Shelley
Czazkowski, Nancy
Daly, Amy
Darmody, Traci
Davis, Wendy Sue
DeBruhl-Phillips, Jan
DeLaughter, Donna
DeMeester, Sue
Denlinger, Lisa
Derlac, Patricia
Dicks, Tamara
Dion, Dawn
Domachowski, Terry
Donnell, Janice
Dose, Tashia
Doyle, Amy
Duffy, Nancy
Dunson, Sharon
D'Ambra, Melissa
Edmiston, Cheri
Edwards, T. Diane
Eifert, Ann
Eliasson, Maureen
Elick, Regina
Ellis, Peggy
Ellis, Julie
Ellis, A.J.
Ely, Renee
Engelhart, Ann
Escandon, Jan
Evensen, Jenifer

Failinger, Gale
Fehr, Ann
Felts, Melinda
Ferrel, Erin McGee
Fleming, Pamela
Fraukimmer, Goma
Freeberg, Dawn
Freeman, Cheryl
Friesen, Donna
Fromholzer, Linda
Fulton, Teri
Gaskins, Lisa
Gehlbach, Sally
Giberson, Karen
Glass, Gail
Goodman, Renee
Gorski, Jeanine
Graf, Amanda
Granberg, Marlene
Grantham, Pat
Gray, Rhonda
Gray Andrea
Green, Peggy
Gregory, Diane
Griffin, Donna
Griffith, Angie
Griggs, Terry
Grinalds, Rhonda
Grob, Pamela
Guardino, Tina
Gustafson, Darcy
Gutknecht, Elizabeth
Hall, Melissa
Hallaway, Kami
Hallmark, Gail
Hamm, Sandy
Hammill, Brenda
Hamp, Teresa
Hanks, Ailene
Hannah, Lesley
Hardin, Sarah Jo
Harris, Lisa
Harshbarger, Rhonda
Haskell, Valerie

Hass, Julie
Hastings, Tami
Haverty, Danna
Heckmaster, Tina
Heinke, Shari
Henderson, Chris
Henkel, Kathy
Hensley, Dawn
Herbert, Rose
Hess, Cindy
Himes, Brenda
Hobelman, Dana
Holm, Valarie
Holzhauer, Kathlene
Hoops, Brenda
Horner, Barb
Horner, Michelle
Horton, Marsha
Hosein, Linda
Howard, Danielle
Huff, Jodi
Hughes,Cherey
Hughes, Wendy
Hunt, Julie
Hurley, Julie
Huyser, Kathy
Iacovelli, Connie
Iannino, Jill
Isner, Cindy
Jackson, Susan
Jackson, Michelle
Jacobsen, Dianne
Jacobson, Kelly
Janser, Jane
Janze, Shelley
Jenkins, Virgina
Jennings, Susan
Jensen, Kathy
Jetton, Teresa
Johns, Roxanne
Johnson, Rona
Johnson, Karen
Jones, Pamela
Jonez, Faye

Kahler, Kelly
Kaiser, Donna
Kallicott, Marian
Kauffman, Dawn
Kellicott, Marian
Kelly, Janice
Kemp, Susan
Kenkel, Kathy
Kennedy, Adele
Key, Sherri
Kieler, Olive
Kikuchi, Ruth
Kindred, Ginny
Kirkpatrick, Lee
Kirsch, Pamela
Kleberg, Lori
Kleet, Karilyn
Klett, Karilyn
Kobza, Cheryl
Kodjz, Stephan
Koop, Dawn
Korzeniewski, Kathleen
Koster, Kathy
Kramer, Tesse
Kramer, Susan
Kyler, Kay Ann
Laimbeer, Elizabeth
Lambert, Darcy
Lamoureux, Connie
Lange, Deb
Langebartels, Kim
Lantz, Theresa
Laucomer, Nancy
Lawler, Kim
Leahy, Mary Fran
Leonard, Stephanie
Letts, Malinda
Lewis, Tammy
Lewis, Kathi
Lind, Cindy
Lindgren, Kathy
Lindquist, Vickie
Lindsey, Chris
Lipps, Crystal

Little, Lisa
Littrell, Belinda
Logan, Joanne
Long, Sheila
Lopen, Sarah
Lowin, Lynda
Lueking, Sarah
Lundberg, Shannon
Lundquist, Annette
Lynxwiler, Verna
Lytton, Cara
MacDonald, Robin
Maier, Beth
Maksim, Alice
Malone, Jennifer
Malosky, Susan
Mangigie, Lisa
Manjeot, Roseann
Marano, Rebecca
Markel, Karen
Marr, Janet
Marshall, Susan
Martlock, Kathy
Masters, Dede
Maughan, Susan
McClelland, Kimberly
McConnell, Cindy
McFarland, Wendy
McGaughey, Anita
McGuire, Sharon
McGuire, Mary
McMahan, Katie
McNabb, Vicki
McNees, Katie
Mikel, Sally
Miller, Nancy
Miller, Laura
Miller, Connie
Miller, Laronda
Miller, Nicole
Mirolli, Maria
Mishler, Robin
Mizuel, Minirer
Moen, Donna L.

Monser, Suzannah
Moore, Delores
Moore, Sue
Moore, Mary
Morris, Debbie
Morris, Dalena
Morrison, Valerie
Morriss, Beverly
Morton, Stephanie
Mucuynski, Marcia
Muro, Teresa
Murphy, Sandy
Murrow, Wayla
Nass, Trish
Nazaroff, Nadie
Neff, Cindy
Negroni, Chris
Nelson, Rochelle
Nelson, Liliana
Nelson, Darla
Nicholson, Vicki
Nieman, Vicki
Nieset, Cheryle
Nix, Karen
Noonan, Sheila
Nusbaum, Joan
Oefinger, Becca
Okerson, Diane
Oleson, Leslie
Orr, Elizabeth
O'Brien, Cindy
Panlener, Carey Lynn
Parish, Sirje
Park, Debbie
Parker, Karen
Parker, Pamela
Parma, Carole
Paternoster, R. Dera
Patlovony, Terry
Paton, Joyce
Payne, Jennifer
Peterson, Anne
Phillips, Karis
Pierson, Jennifer

Pitfield, Renae
Plotts, Nancy
Pointz, Rebecca
Pollum, Amy
Poolener, Carey Lynn
Prohoroff, Irene
Pugh, Tami
Quinnell, Susan
Radic, Shelly
Rashid, Julie
Reeves, Dianna
Regan, Marilyn
Revell, Wendy
Rezan, Marilyn
Richmond, Jennifer
Riegle, Julie
Rinehart, Charlene
Ritzheim, Julie
Rizkalla, Kathy
Roadhouse, Mary
Rochelle, Marvin
Rodgers, Elizabeth
Rodriquez, Stephanis
Rogers, Barb
Ronning, Linda
Rose, Susan
Ross, Debbie
Rotley, Dawn
Rowe, Leslie
Roynon, Nancy
Rubeck, Kathy
Ruchti, Lynda
Sabo, Kari
Sacco, Lori Ann
Salvant, Janna
Sansern, Jewel
Sassman, Christy
Saucy, Stephanie
Sayre, Mary
Sbory, Karen
Schick, Georgine
Schilinski, Carol
Schlein, Michelle
Schmitt, Dana

Schoenbarn, Connie
Schrock, Jennifer
Schroeder, Pam
Schuemann, Liane
Schultz, Elaine
Schwartz, Carolyn
Scott, Charlene
Scruitsky, Renee
Seguin, Pan
Sewell, Laurie
Shippel, Lois
Shirk, Lucy
Shoemaker, Gina
Shufflebarger, Dierdre
Sible, Rebecca
Sidney, Sharon
Skeans, Kim
Skoglund, Ardis
Slough, Diane
Small, SallySmith,
Mary Jo
Smith, Sharon
Smith, Pat
Smith, Kristi
Smith, Carrie
Snook, Karol
Snyder, Ramona
Sorensen, Peggy
Spada, Becky
Stahlman, Gayle
Stanford, Karen
Stepien, Cheryl
Stevens, Debbie
Stewart, Peggy
Stokes, Ellen
Stony, Janey
Stouffer, Gayle
Straley, Janneth
Susich, Donalee
Sweeney, Vonda
Tackman, Heidi
Taylor, Pam
Teel, Kari
Theander, Danielle

Thompson, Penny
Tobin, Lorraine M.
Tucker, Penny
Turchik, Cindi
Turice, Rose
Tyson, Rachel
Ulmer, Andrea
Vandeberghe, Monica
VanMaanen, Shari
VanPietten, Amy
Villalobos, Audrey
Visca, Kelley
Vizzachero, Chris
VonKleeck, Karen
Wagner, Tamara
Waidelich, Eileen
Wall, Tonia
Walsh, Mary
Watson, Theresa
Webb, Kam
Weber, Kathryn
Wefel, Chris
Wellers, Heather
Wenrich, Julie
Whaley, Margie
Whipkey, Tracey
Wicker, Jane
Wilburn, Ercel
Williams, Sue
Williams, Heather
Wills, Jean
Wilson, Michelle
Wilson, Rae Jean
Winston, Patsy
Winters, Marcy
Witzki, Stacy
Wollner, Meg
Wurst, Patsy
Wyse, Julia
Ziegler, Patricia
Zuber, Ginny
Zweidinger, Melanie

Index

❰ MOPS IS. . . . ❱

MOPS stands for Mothers of Preschoolers, a program designed to encourage mothers with children under school age through relationships and resources. These women come from different backgrounds and lifestyles, yet have similar needs and a shared desire to be the best mothers they can be!

A MOPS group provides a caring, accepting atmosphere for today's mother of preschoolers. Here she has an opportunity to share concerns, explore areas of creativity, and hear instruction that equips her for the responsibilities of family and community. The MOPS group also includes MOPPETS, a loving, learning experience for children.

Approximately 2,700 groups meet in churches throughout the United States, Canada, and 19 other countries, to meet the needs of more than 100,000 women. Many more mothers are encouraged by MOPS resources, including *MOMSense* radio and magazine, MOPS' web site, and publications such as this book.

Find out how MOPS International can help you become part of the MOPS♥to♥Mom Connection.

MOPS International
P.O. Box 102200
Denver, CO 80250-2200
Phone 1-800-929-1287 or 303-733-5353
E-mail: Info@MOPS.org
Web site: http://www.MOPS.org

To learn how to start a MOPS group,
call 1-888-910-MOPS.
For MOPS products call The MOPShop
1-888-545-4040.

Check out these other great resources from MOPS!

The Mom's Devotional Bible

Moms, you don't have to go it alone! *The Mom's Devotional Bible* is a companion and trusted source of wisdom to help you along the path of mothering. A full year of weekday devotions written by Elisa Morgan, president of MOPS (Mothers of Preschoolers) International, are combined with Bible text to offer you and moms everywhere fresh perspective on topics such as time management, mentors for moms, sibling rivalry, and much more. And on weekends, find new insight as you explore "special interest" areas like "A Mother's Legacy," "Train Up a Child," "A Time to Play," and "Get Growing!"

The complete text of the best-selling New International Version provides accuracy you can trust. A list of resources in the back of the Bible shows you where to turn for help with special challenges you face as a mother. And from family traditions to praying for young children, twenty full-color pages add a warm, keepsake touch. *The Mom's Devotional Bible*—get yours today!

Hardcover: 0-310-92501-0
Softcover: 0-310-92422-7

A wide selection of Mom's Devotional Bible gift products are also available.

What Every Child Needs
Getting to the Heart of Mothering

ELISA MORGAN & CAROL KUYKENDALL

The love you have for your children can give them a foundation for life—provided you show it in the ways they need it most. And now there's help from the people best qualified to give it: moms like you who are successfully meeting the challenge.

What Every Child Needs draws on the insights of moms across the United States and on the latest research to help you meet your children's nine basic needs for:

- **Security:** Hold-Me-Close Love
- **Affirmation:** Crazy-About-Me Love
- **Belonging:** Fit-Me-into-the-Family Love
- **Discipline**: Give-Me-Limits Love
- **Guidance:** Show-Me-and-Tell-Me Love
- **Respect**: Let-Me-Be-Me Love

- **Play:** Play-With-Me Love
- **Independence:** Let-Me-Grow-Up Love
- **Hope:** Give-Me-Hope Love

Using a child's language of love, the authors show you how to recognize and meet each need . . . and how to respect your own needs in the process.

Hardcover: 0-310-21151-4
Audio Pages: 0-310-21579-X

What Every Mom Needs
Meet Your Nine Basic Needs (and Be a Better Mom)

ELISA MORGAN &
CAROL KUYKENDALL

If you enjoyed *What Every Child Needs*, you'll love its best-selling companion! In *What Every Mom Needs* Elisa Morgan and Carol Kuykendall of MOPS International point the way to relief and fulfillment in the midst of motherhood's hectic pace. After more than twenty years of research and experience with moms, MOPS has identified your nine basic needs as a mother: significance, identity, growth, intimacy, instruction, help, recreation, perspective, and hope. *What Every Mom Needs* is an invaluable resource for women who long to expand their personal horizons and become better mothers at the same time.

Hardcover: 0-310-20097-0
Softcover: 0-310-21920-5
Audio Pages: 0-310-20417-8

A Mother's Footprints of Faith
Stories of Hope and Encouragement

CAROL KUYKENDALL

Using poignant and humorous anecdotes, Carol Kuykendall shares the value of perspective in the midst of motherhood's frantic pace. She truthfully illustrates how God often uses difficult situations to draw you closer to himself. Join Carol as she reflects on her own journey. She will help you discover wealth in the footprints leading up to where you stand now and find guidance for the rest of the journey.

Hardcover: 0-310-21083-6

Ask for these and other MOPS products at your favorite Christian bookstore.

ZONDERVAN™

GRAND RAPIDS, MICHIGAN 49530 USA

WWW.ZONDERVAN.COM

We want to hear from you. Please send your comments about this book to us in care of the address below. Thank you.

GRAND RAPIDS, MICHIGAN 49530 USA

WWW.ZONDERVAN.COM